Kling Lindquist

Kling Lindquist
The Realm of Shadows

Preface by
Bradford White Fiske
Introduction by
Mario Pisani

Editorial Director USA
Pierantonio Giacoppo

Chief Editor of Collection
Maurizio Vitta

Publishing Coordinator
Franca Rottola

Graphic Design
Paola Polastri

Editing
Martyn Anderson

Colour-separation
Litofilms Italia, Bergamo

Printing
Poligrafiche Bolis, Bergamo

First published October 2000

ISBN 88-7838-077-6

Contents

The Realm of Shadows

by Bradford White Fiske

We understand architecture in terms of its reflections: as signification that contains but transcends the function it involves; as representation of society's ideals and conversely of its fears; as manifestation of something other than itself—be that the power of an institution or the idea of a god; as a mirror of what is believed to be known.

We understand shadows as elements of reflection: comparative darkness, but specifically that from and of an object; corresponding or reiterative imagery; symbols and prefigurations; the intimation of something not entirely known.

We think of architecture as if it were an instrument of language: texts to be read, and from the reading to ultimately realize the attendant layers of meaning and multiplicities of metaphor; semiology to be studied.

We think of shadows as visual elements of poetry: oddly immobile testimonies to that which exists; form that, though devoid of substance, is ripe with implication and potential; expressions of interpretation rather than of recording.

We, as architects, identify with architecture more as process than object—process that concerns itself with the production of both structure and meaning—meaning that is ultimately partially revealed by the object itself.

We identify with shadows with similar duality—as projection, as stated, but also as darkness connoting both the tranquility of refuge and the apprehension of the unknown.

Both architecture and shadows are about representation of something other than itself. Shadows exist adjacent to or verging on, but not coincident with, their source; they define an area where one is not. Architecture exists only where it goes beyond the limitations of simply referring to its purpose or program; where building becomes more than simply its determinants. We engage in architecture both inspired and rewarded by parallel and paradoxical expectations to reflect, respond, and reiterate; but we embrace architecture to pursue moments of poetic transformation. We practice architecture within the realm of shadows.

Many of the shadows cast within the city of Philadelphia ethereally record the fifty-three years of our history. The patterns of light and dark that play upon the streets and plazas of the city's center are visual testimony of the firm's influence and contribution. In 1969, during the period of both growth and reestablishment, Vincent Kling spoke to the essence of our endeavors:

"When we build we are telling the world what we stand for. Our structures will influence our lives for a very long time. The choices we have in hand to achieve this influence are legion; no longer is it a simple matter of bricks and mortar, windows and doors. New methods, new systems and a seemingly endless demand from more and more people give the designer fascinating opportunities at every turn…

Our fundamental conviction in approaching the design of every project is that architecture is for people…the greatest challenge to the architect is to recreate environments for people…Elegance, grace, style, functional efficiency, economy and durability are still as important to owners as ever, but today the most pressing need is for humane spaces in which people can live and breathe".

Founded on the tenets of modernism and invested in the issues of humanism, the firm that has evolved over the years is in no small part a projection of that which it once was; and influences of previous generations remain clearly visible in our current work. There are a great many explorations and actualizations in our past from which we take pride; and more important, from which we continue to learn.

The works included in this edition constitute an overview of our practice during the past decade and represent both a continuum and a departure from that which preceded. The architecture presented simultaneously reiterates the body of history from which it has been cast and exists as that aspect of shadow that signifies a remnant from which the substance has departed; phantasms to which we have the opportunity and responsibility to bring new meaning and worth.

This period has been noteworthy for the technological sophistication required in the resolution of many of our assignments—an architecture that reflects science, safety, and systems. At the same time, over these ten years, we have focused on a paramount concern for interaction and the enhancement of collaboration. Our task has been to bring together disparate groups within a building or campus, and to create an environment conducive to the often contradictory requirements of people and processes.

There exist, as important aspects of our practice, concerns that reflect the diversity of our people and the complexity of the problems we are asked to address. There is great regard for careful integration of the rational order that is established by understanding building usage and the supporting systems of structure and servicing. Our architecture has always been faced with the task of helping human beings establish control over their environment, but there is an attendant issue embodied in our approach focused on preserving the environment concurrent with its willful adaptation.

During the decade, we have been asked to expand our architecture to an unprecedented number of new clients—and their unprecedented and often undefined needs. Our buildings are reflections of these requests. Unburdened by a singular vocabulary, we have been free to explore architecture based upon issues; and the buildings realized have been derived from the process of making architecture—from discovery, collaboration, and culture.

Our work has ranged and continues to range dramatically in appearance, experience, and scale, but it is consistently founded in a need to interrogate, analyze, and criticize. Our buildings attempt to reconcile the many contradictory demands placed upon them without the sacrifice of artistry for expediency. Our process asks for the active participation of our clients and our team, while striving to reach the level of symbolic discourse articulated by culture as a whole.

As I write this introduction, a number of the represented projects are just finishing construction; and although their respective dialogues with light and shadow speak to their different characters of enclosure, each is intended to exemplify a sophisticated synthesis of the possibilities of context and the culture of the client. These buildings exist as tapestries that give evidence of both intention and

approach, but it is work whose ultimate meaning is discovered only from direct observation and from true understanding of its relationship to its surroundings.

There are, among our recent work, buildings that aspire to capture characteristics and experiences afforded by the paintings of DeChirico; to offer, from the materiality of their design, clear boundaries; yet from within this realm of limitation, to present the likelihood of transgression. The architecture of Dow Jones and Merck 800, for all the consideration paid to pattern and patina, derives its greatest validation from the celebration of shadow and its suggestion.

Still other of our latest designs endeavor to disavow physical separation, relying instead on pervasive transparency to provide the foundation of experience, and borrowing vistas from the surrounding environment as elements of the architectural composition. Within the building for SAP America and the designs for Shenzhen, the projection of skeletal tracery painted across the floorplates becomes seemingly more substantial than the aluminum and steel elements themselves. And on the exterior surface of these buildings, the interplay of daylight and glass causes shifts in perception as transparency and reflectivity battle for momentary supremacy—and awareness is constantly reinformed by the object's metamorphoses.

After fifty-three years, we have arrived at a time of redefinition, aspiring not only for new challenges to address, but also for greater expectations that we must labor to realize. We will enter the next century committed to reaching beyond present limitations, but holding on to our

propensity to perceive beauty in darkness. For it is within the realm of shadows that the probability of poetic transformation most clearly exists.

Security, calmness, and profundity

by Mario Pisani

The most striking thing about the most recent works of architecture designed by the Kling Lindquist firm, even upon a quick initial analysis, is the way they express a sense of strength and security, calmness, and profundity; in a word: real majesty.

The firm we are talking about is a well-organised and highly qualified team that began working just after the war, designing such interesting works as Phoenixville Hospital (1951); the Radio Corporation of America offices in Cherry Hill, NJ (1955); the Triangle Publication, Inc. in Philadelphia, PA (1963); and the Merrill Lynch Building in Princeton, NJ (1985).

The firm's most recent architecture has moved beyond the borders of the United States to settle, with careful awareness, into different parts of the planet: the United Kingdom, France, China, Japan and, of course, plenty of other works in their homeland. These works show attention to tradition and their surroundings while expressing constant tension towards high-tech and the most up-to-date issues of contemporary design. Anyway, whatever style or features Kling Lindquist adopt for their buildings, they always transmit a sense of security, calmness, and profundity of thought. This concept could be interpreted as an updating of what Vitruvius - the first scholar of architectural theory whose writings have been handed down to us from Roman times - describes as firmitas, classifying it as one of the key components of the art of building. This aspect of architecture seems to be deeply entrenched in the design and construction techniques of a country like the United States with such huge resources at its disposal.

The projects in question, notably the TV Center and Cultural Center both in Shenzhen, China, show stimulating signs of research, experimentation, and slow but progressive changes in stylistic idiom right at the cutting-edge of contemporary architectural design. In other works, these signs are less showy or striking than the hype the deconstructivists have publicised through the media; they are much more cautious signs, often hidden away underground or projected into the mental realms of prospective clients - whose financial backing is of crucial importance in the process of constructing architecture.

There is a sort of unifying thread running right through Kling Lindquist's wide range of stylistically elaborate works: pharmaceutical research centres, university departments, or even skyscrapers and commercial-business centres, all work around the idea of renewal through continuity in the great tradition of first the Modern Movement and then the International Style, drawing on a style of artistry capable of exploiting opportunities to the full. I am referring in particular to the Bayer AG building in Kyoto, Japan, a powerfully compact construction brimming with artistic force and capable of bringing together Western and Japanese culture; Glaxo Inc. in Research Triangle Park in North Carolina, certainly one of the firm's most successful and intriguing works of architecture; and, most significantly, the strangely unique image of the dynamically intriguing SAP America project in Newtown Square, Pennsylvania. The same basic features can also be found in the Bell Atlantic headquarters in Philadelphia, Pennsylvania, and of course the TV Center and Cultural Center, both in

Shenzhen, that have already been mentioned.

These works of architecture seem to grasp the sense of what the italian critic Claudio Magris states in his book Utopia and Disenchantment, Stories, Hopes and Illusions of the Modern Movement, where he claims that "On the threshold of the year 2000, there is no pathos associated with the idea of reaching the end, just a deep sense of a radical change in society and mankind in general and hence the sense of the end, not of the world, but of a secular way of experiencing, imagining, and managing it." Kling Lindquist's best works of architecture manage to sense all this and pass it on accurately to anybody observing them.

For instance, in working out the design for the QVC in West Goshen, Pennsylvania, the architects initially came up with a number of possible ideas for the precise purpose of exploring quite unconventional realms, incorporating transgressive or highly unusual features, like for example the idea of replacing one single roof with a number of small conic, billowing tent-like roofs. Another idea developed at the drawing board stage involved replacing a conventional wall with transparent glass, lacerating them with perpendicular glass partitions that extend out into the semi-rural environment. A third design created an imaginative interior fitted out with a jungle-gym-like superstructure. A fourth design divided up the interior along the lines of urban planning, with streets and square etc. Needless to say, the final design mirrors all the various ideas toyed with, and when it is eventually constructed the building will transmit that feeling of comfort, privacy, elegance, and originality the architects and clients were looking for.

The first thing we sense when confronting architecture like Glaxo Wellcome plc. in Stevenage, Hertfordshire, in Great Britain; Merck & Co. Inc. at West Point, PA, Thomas Jefferson University (Lewis J. Bluemle Jr. Life Sciences Building) in Philadelphia; or Drexel University built in the same city, is that feeling of firmitas or calm ornamentation, a gloss of refined elegance without overdoing things or trying to astound, just the idea of passing on a feeling of comfort and well-being. The second thing worth pointing out, because it shows up in all the Kling Lindquist firm's projects, even in its distinctly urban skyscrapers, is the way they manage to interact in a highly balanced and intriguing manner with the environment or rather with the natural surroundings, the places where they are built. In works like the Philadelphia Office Tower and Bell Atlantic Headquarters, also in Philadelphia, there are real traces of a historical feeling of belonging, conjuring up a sense of place and creating new spaces that become important parts of the city fabric.

For example, our architects studied and designed a pedestrian sculpture-plaza for Thomas Jefferson University, which marks a new boundary between the university district and the residential neighbourhood skillfully blending the imposing campus building into the city in terms of both scale and character.

Kling Lindquist clearly wanted to draw on the resources of Japanese tradition in the project designed for Bayer in Kyoto, notably using technology that pays careful attention to nature and to context in general, so as to reconcile the new presence with the nearby residential districts. All the

windows overlook green landscaping, drawing on it as an essential aspect of the overall design. An extensive Japanese garden envelops the building and a bit further on there is a thick wood of bamboo trees. The lower section contains another garden in the middle and bright pavilions are spread throughout the surroundings.

This "green" or "eco-friendly" approach is explained by Kling Lindquist's keen awareness of the rapidly spreading symptoms of a general loss of sense of place; the danger of all differences being cancelled out and everything eventually looking the same, the suburbs of Tokyo being indistinguishable from those of Paris, the outskirts of Philadelphia looking just like Hong Kong. The idea of urban settlements as places that spring up in the midst of and in symbiosis with nature, interacting together to everybody's benefit, is likely to disappear as metropolitan chaos spreads everywhere. Even our urban landmarks are in danger of disappearing: those key architectural features that have always been landmarks of civil life right through the history of human civilisation, capable of instilling individuals with a sense of identity and belonging. A place has its own easily identifiable space with its own peculiar character making it stand out from all the rest. Ever since Greek civilisation and Roman times, people have always believed in the existence of a genius loci or spirit that inhabited a place and which had to be measured up to, understood, and communicated with in order to operate in that space. Designing architecture meant visualising as clearly as possible that spirit, or in other words architects were expected to design places full of meaning where people could work in peace, enjoy themselves or just inhabit the space. Quoting Hölderlin's couplet: "Deservedly so and yet / poetically, man Inhabits the earth".

Drawing on their innate talent, Kling Lindquist create a particularly successful bond between nature and architecture, between buildings, trees, plants, water, and open spaces. In this approach to architecture, they seem particularly aware of the theory Martin Heidegger expressed in his master piece Interrupted Paths. The German philosopher writes that: "My master told me: 'Nature is the inspiration, the only truth, and perhaps the support behind all human activities. But do not represent nature the way those landscape artists do, showing us nothing but its outside appearance! Inquire into its causes, the reason for its forms, its vital growth....' This taught me about the flowers - inside and outside - the shapes and colours of birds; I realised how trees grow and how they stand up to storms. The water cycle: rain, evaporation, snow, storms".

In addition to nature, which co-exists and grows with buildings, as epitomized by QVC in Pennsylvania, Bayer AG in Kyoto, and Glaxo Inc. in North Carolina, space also has an important part to play, that sort of "air cushion" that envelops, protects and, most significantly, exalts such constructions as the United States Food and Drug Administration in White Oak, Maryland, the QVC Corporate Facility in West Goshen, Pennsylvania, and also Bayer AG in Kyoto, designed to be a sort of Acropolis buried in nature, and last of all Glaxo Inc. in Research Triangle Park, North Carolina, a building

simulating a city with its own roads, squares, and congregation places where people exchange glances. Here we can quite obviously see the influence of Frank Lloyd Wright, who pointed out in The Natural House that "Space must be seen as architecture, otherwise there is no architecture.....; it is in the very nature of an organic building to grow out of its own location, emerge from the earth and come to light - the earth itself has always been an essential part of a building. And so we have the maximum expression of this new ideal of a building as something organic. A building that imposes itself like a tree in the midst of nature".

All that: relation to space and nature in Kling Lindquist's works of architecture is designed to create a sense of man's identity in relation to place, but also his sense of disorientation. Both of these are primary elements in man's presence on Earth. Christian Norberg-Schulz reminds us that "While identification is the basis of man's sense of belonging to a place, orientation turns him into that homo viator which is part of his nature. It is a characteristic of man to have exalted his own nomadic nature for such a long time; he wanted to be free to conquer the world. We are now beginning to realise that real freedom requires a sense of belonging, and that "inhabiting" means belonging to a concrete place".

In the seventies and eighties architecture began to tackle large scale projects constructed in both urban and non-urban contexts and developed out of the constraints associated with new building types like research centres and universities, hospital complexes, business-management centres, and spin-doctoring centres working the image-making industry. The

emergence of such needs often coincides with progress in research into new experimental and settlement models guiding operations focusing on problems associated with the new scale of town-planning, examining the issue of founding settlement models based on comparisons with contextual geographic conditions. These new settlements, small strongholds of science, are often designed around some sort of "dam" or "bridge" which, as in other times in history - take for instance the Roman aqueducts or huge walls like the Great Wall of China or Hadrian's Wall on the Scottish border - mark the land by the way they express the need to interpret a geographical-settlement situation, also capable of gauging the latest scale of building and the nature of their surroundings.

Almost all of the Kling Lindquist firm's recent works of architecture bear the marks of building "big", but scale is particularly relevant and evident in certain particular designs. In these cases, we are almost entitled to say that building on a large scale adds to, develops, and even exalts architectural design. Take, for example, Glaxo France's Administration Headquarters in Marly-le-Roi, where a gently sloping hill is marked with five buildings of identical size. The buildings slope downwards creating an intriguing skyline, while a number of gardens landscaped with different species of plants are slotted inside closed courtyards, following a pleasant flow of water injecting a nice sense of freshness into the surroundings.

The architecture shows an interest in the work of the New York Five and, above all, Richard Meier, but there is also a subtle vein of seduction running through the wide glass surfaces hiding the elliptical-shaped stairwell suspended in space.

Sterling Winthrop Inc., a complex designed for pharmaceutical research located in Upper Providence Township in Pennsylvania, has a decidedly specular site plan separated by a sloping axis, a real high-level landscape joining together the heart of the site plan constructed around twin structures with a peripheral addition. Everything is buried in greenery and witnesses to a cool approach to research work aimed at improving and dilating human life.

The architecture works around brick which, quoting what Marguerite Yourcenar writes in Adriano's Memoires, is that "eternal stone that slowly returns to the earth from which it came, and whose yielding and imperceptible crumbling happens in such a way that the building remains a volume, even when it has ceased to be fortress, circus, tomb".

The headquarters of the United States Food and Drug Administration in White Oak, Maryland, is a really solid structure, a sort of administration citadel constructed out of a careful combination of modular blocks designed to bring out the way solid structures and spaces interact, and how built space is related to the natural environment surrounding it and enveloping it completely, instilling architecture with that feeling of well-being and calmness we mentioned at the beginning. Upon closer examination, we can see that the site plan is a homage to mannerism and in particular to Piazza Campidoglio designed by Michelangelo, which is here reproduced in a trapezium shape extending from the entrance to the central building. The path towards the centre of the site plan is injected with

dynamism by differences between the sloping elevations allowing glimpses of the landscaped courtyards. This sort of administrative Campidoglio alludes to a need for control and direction, and the fact that these functions derive from the architecture tells us this project is designed to consciously work towards a better quality of human life.

In line with the main trends on the international architectural scene over the last few decades, the term "High Tech" does not so much refer to a style as to a certain approach to design, a mental attitude of a certain group of architects sharing the same basic tenets and artistic awareness.

In the early 1970s architecture found itself confronted with constant innovation in building systems and engineering in general, that ended up favoring a subtle taste for showing off new forms of technology, particularly those involving glass and steel, almost in deliberate contrast with conventional building using reinforced concrete. In the early days, this approach resulted in the construction of simple buildings but, as time went by, these works gradually became more intricate, gaining a form of stylistic maturity and artistic autonomy embodied in a number of design principles. Large undivided spaces have been constructed serving a variety of different purposes; the "skin" of buildings is accentuated as a means of mediating between the artificial environment on the inside and the external environment on the outside; a kind of monumental rendering of stairways and vertical connections gradually took shape, as epitomized, for instance, in the Beaubourg building.

SAP America also shows a love for the natural landscape and attention to

new forms of technology. The building's function as a business centre called for a special design in harmony with its site location and a certain awareness of its picturesque surroundings featuring tall trees and other important species of plants. This resulted in the construction of a linear, winding construction opening up views of the surrounding trees. Technology appears in the "nature-inspired" green-coloured windows looking out onto the surroundings that adapt perfectly to changes in the seasons and the gradual passage of time throughout the course of the day. They also help tone down the geometric form of the entire building.

The underlying goal behind Kling Lindquist's design for the headquarters of Glaxo in the Research Triangle Park was to knit this new highly high-tech complex into surrounding nature: an area full of large pine forests. The project was supposed to express a positive image with clear but also elegant allusions to ecology. A combination that holds together an image of efficiency and elegance with an exaltation of the values of nature. This same line of thinking lies behind the construction of an artificial lake, carefully placed in relation to the building. All this helps project an image of efficiency, easy for the media to communicate, as well as a feasible idea of the building of the future.

The project for a TV Center in Shenzhen shows just what elegantly cultured results technology can produce. Kling Lindquist has designed, a Center for the Arts in the same city, drawing on the natural force of the local landscape as a means of establishing a hierarchy of program components and spatial sequences. There is a library holding four million books, a 4000-seat concert hall, a music museum, a facility for hosting conferences and public events, various areas designed for leisure and entertainment purposes, and a shopping mall. All this well away from traffic, as if it were a world apart, opening up onto a monumental plaza with a really large artificial lake designed along traditional Chinese lines. Here water evokes peacefulness, the kind of calmness that encourages reading and intellectual thought, away from the hustle and bustle of everyday life. This project is like a kind of secular cathedral or, better still, a shrine to the modern city in the most noble sense of the word. Throughout this century a presence like this, in harmony with Western tradition, has provided the city with a sort of beating heart, a centre where our society can reflect on the past and on history, as well as indulging in an enjoyable pastime. This is not just the home of culture, it is also a source of simple, humble entertainment for everybody. This creates what Ernst Juger has described as the modern museum impulse or in other words "a tendency to place living things inside somewhere motionless and unassailable, and perhaps also the desire to compile a huge catalogue of material, carefully ordered with meticulous precision so that our descendants will have an accurate picture of our life and all its ramified interests". The purpose is obvious: to live on through the objects we loved or which were quite simply important to us, objects capable of talking about us, our tastes and general sensibility.

A modern-day critic, Jean Clair, has pointed out that this is why "nowadays, museums are gaining ground rather in the same way our deserts are growing:

they occupy the space life abandons, and like well-meaning pirates they raid the wrecks it leaves behind".

We would like to conclude this journey through certain works of architecture that have stimulated our interest with a quote from the french historical Georges Duby who said: "Despite what people think, they still enjoy a narrative, myth or legend; in a word, they love a good story (...) I think what they like about a story, as they project themselves into it, is the way it reassures them that they are living a life, that this whirl of sudden jumps and ineffable tropisms, all these partial glances and incomplete movements, these transient words that do not belong to them and just trip off their tongues, all this anonymous multiplicity in the midst of a passing day, a day like all the rest, before opening a book that they have decided to read that evening; that all this, as in the book, will some day come together and make a life, however meaningless it might be: a life in the telling, a fate".

Kling Lindquist has certainly told us some comforting stories, stories which are much more intriguing than the few excerpts I have gathered together here. That is why I hope the remarks I have made will at least encourage readers to visit these places and actually experience the emotions they conjure up. In other words, I hope you will listen for yourself to the stories they have to tell.

Works

Drexel University
Bennet S. LeBow Engineering Center
Center of Automation Technology
Philadelphia, Pennsylvania

This award winning Engineering Center project is notably successful in two special aspects: it gives Drexel University a gateway to the campus for the first time in its more than 100-year history, and it celebrates Drexel's strength and reputation in the fields of contemporary engineering research. The use of bright terra-cotta brick reflects the color and material utilized throughout Drexel's campus (as distinguished from the darker brick of the adjacent University of Pennsylvania campus). Glazing with steel mullions and exposed ducts and vent stacks communicate and dramatize the presence of high technology.

Although a relatively modestly sized facility of 126,000 SF (11,700 SM), the two-building complex is packed with a variety of labs for high-technology research: ceramics, composite material, robotics, photolithography, biosensor and catalysis and reaction engineering. A secured area designed to support behavioral simulation work is located in the basement.

The design placed all laboratories facing the street where passersby can look in on facilities, equipment and activities. Faculty offices and student spaces are grouped around an interior landscaped courtyard, which provides sheltered exposure for interaction and contemplation. The building mass around this popular courtyard is stepped to maximize solar penetration. Constantly alive with pedestrians, the sequence of entry events from Market Street, Philadelphia's major east-west artery, through an arcaded portal to the sun-drenched courtyard, embodies the true meaning of experiencing architecture.

The 68,000 SF (6,300 SM) Bennett S. LeBow Engineering Center includes 16,145 SF (1,500 SM) for materials engineering; a 14,000 SF (1,300 SM) specialty research center; CADD and other computer facilities; and 5,600 SF (520 SM) of classrooms, offices, and various support systems.

The Center for Automation Technology is a 58,000 SF (5,400 SM) five-story building functioning both as a flexible research laboratory and as an area for demonstrating ongoing research from 19 different laboratories on campus. Additionally, the building houses an integrated automation suite with a manufacturing test cell; biochemical engineering; catalysis and reaction engineering laboratories; and semiconductor engineering with clean rooms.

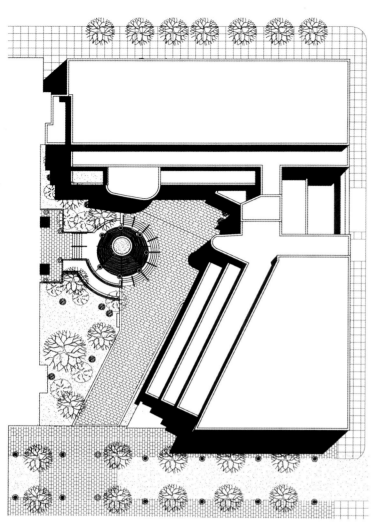

As identified by the roof plan and images, the engineering building establishes a strong street wall, which while defining the site's boundary also presents with its colonnade an important gateway to Drexel's campus.

The two glass enclosed stairwells not only act as important figural elements within the composition, but afford focused views of the courtyard.

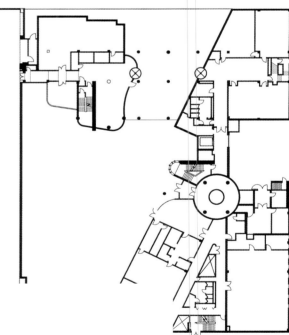

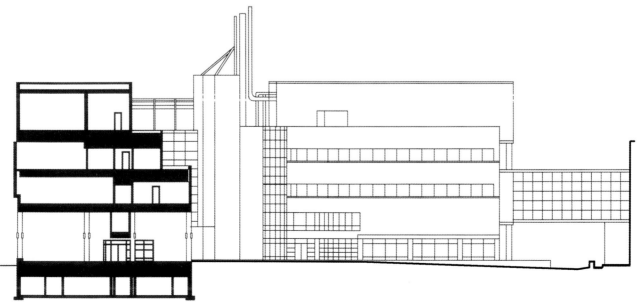

Bell Atlantic Corporation Headquarters Tower
Philadelphia, Pennsylvania

Within the orthogonal grid of Philadelphia, the grand diagonal of the Benjamin Franklin Parkway is important not only as a vehicular and pedestrian boulevard, but also as a primary urban vista. The 1,370,000 SF (127,000 SM), 53-story Bell Atlantic Tower is set in front of Logan Circle, the heart of the Parkway, and imparts a major presence in the city's skyline.

The principal challenges were to create a high profile corporate presence for Bell Atlantic, while honoring the covenants of city zoning ordinances, rightfully protective of the esteemed location. Setbacks required for buildings of this height of 230 feet from the centerline of the parkway contributed to the genesis of the design, coupled with an overriding awareness of the context. Resolution entailed massing the building to the south of the site, with an elegant urban plaza extending out to the parkway and the landscaped fountain of Logan Circle. Thus, the south and west faces of the tower continue the strong street edge which typifies the city's fabric. The plaza and park also work to bridge the two urban contexts.

In addition to satisfying requirements for efficiency, leasability and context, the tower design most directly addressed client needs and concerns. The massing acknowledges the architectural traditions of the area while providing a singular identity for the corporate owner. Imperial red granite from Sweden was used to recall and honor the brick so prevalent throughout Philadelphia's history, and the plaza continues the fabric of urban parks interlaced throughout the city.

The building is stepped back at the top to heighten its verticality and to create terraces; at night, the crown is lit to create a waterfall of light against the night sky. The faceted design provides a high percentage of perimeter area and full-height office windows frame spectacular views of the city.

The 45,000 SF (4,200 SM) granite-paved pedestrian plaza, with 300-car parking garage and the tower, features a circular reflecting fountain which provides a transition between the Benjamin Franklin Parkway and the building's entrance. A monumental three-story glass portal framed in granite extends into the interior public areas. The double-height lobby features polychrome marble walls and floors, accented with polished and satin bronze. Close attention to interior detailing adds to the building's richness; for example, distinctive ceiling features include opalescent glass chandeliers and perimeter cove lighting.

The Bell Atlantic Tower's form and surfaces were to convey not only an aura of stateliness, contributing to the building's inhabitants, but appropriateness to the architectural traditions of Philadelphia. Within a cityscape recently growing dense with cool, glass objects, the granite-clad design was to embody dignity.

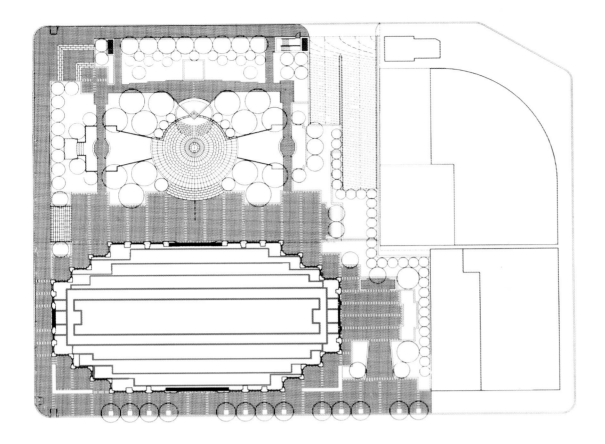

The one acre granite and landscaped plaza on the tower's north side not only mediates between the pedestrian environment of Logan Circle and the urban fabric of the city to the south; but establishes the primary publicly identified entrance.

The tower floor plans gradually evolve in order to present a gracious massing to the city of Philadelphia. The cladding of red Swedish granite implies a singular warmth to the skyline.

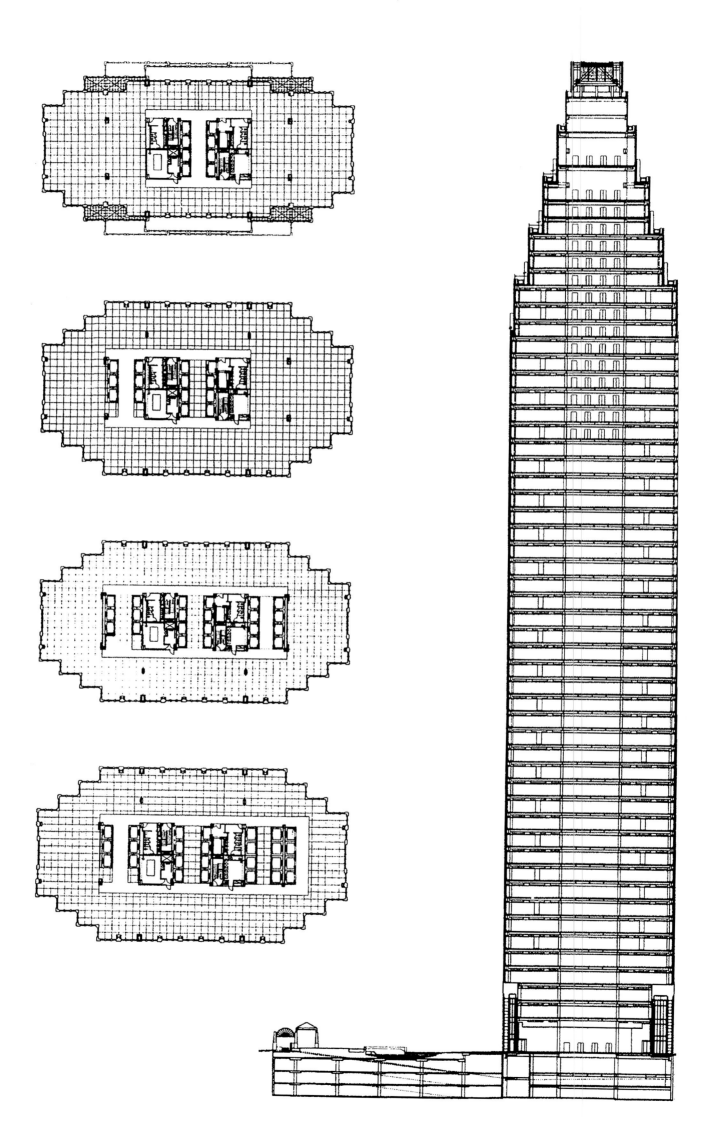

Marble from Portugal, Turkey and Italy are composed to provide a rich and directional lobby. Details of the interface between the stone and the bronze accents have been carefully composed.

Bayer AG
Pharmaceutical Research Center
Kyoto, Japan

A design competition required 70,000 SM (750,000 SF) of space for a Pharmaceutical Research Center on a 2.72 hectare (4 acre) site. The prominence of the setting was significant in the development of an image that would reflect both Japanese culture and technology.

Site issues of context, nature, and physical presence contributed to the design solution. Adjacent residential neighborhoods influenced the scale of massing and the use of landscaping to soften the presence of the complex.

The core of the landscaping is in the tradition of formal Japanese garden design, with transitory edges that allow the site to blend naturally into the surrounding bamboo forest. Six five-story research buildings were designed as increments of phased construction.

Oriented around a central garden and water court, the complex positions common spaces in pavilions within the park-like setting. Locating two levels of parking, service areas and the central utility plant to underground construction further contributed to optimizing the natural environment.

Design of the laboratory units utilizes a simple cubic form with vertical exhaust risers and external emergency walkways. Stainless steel cladding is intended to express the enclosed technology, while softened roof lines and gridded pavilions indigenous forms.

Programmatic elements of laboratory facility requirements, allowing for biology research growth, accommodating handling of diverse materials, and incremental parking growth were important elements of the design resolution. The 8,000 SM (86,000 SF) components of laboratory module growth provided the basic framework within which aesthetic and programmatic decisions occurred.

The aerial perspective
and site plans speak to
the careful integration
of the seven buildings
in the existing bamboo
forest and the
consideration given to
the steep site
contouring.

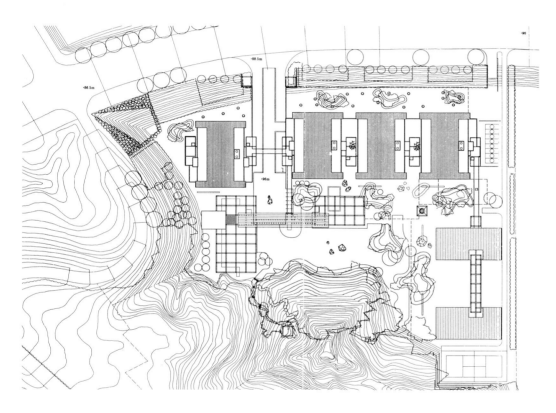

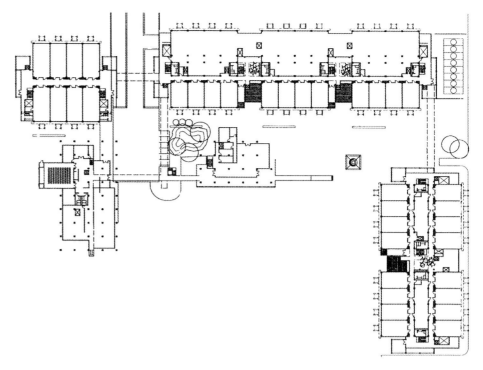

While the section and elevation indicate the relationship between architecture and environment, the two model photographs present the complex as understood at arrival or from the adjacent residential neighborhood.

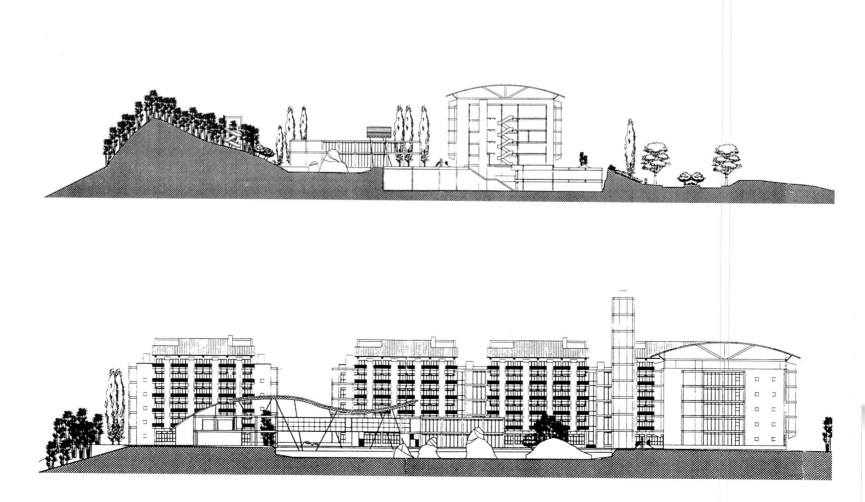

Thomas Jefferson University Lewis J. Bluemle Jr. Life Sciences Building
Philadelphia, Pennsylvania

A variety of vertical elements are accentuated with the deliberate intent to heighten this 289,000 SF (27,000 SM) modular graduate research laboratory building located on a mere half city block. The sculpture plaza entrance and forecourt on the west helps the building to define the boundary between the institutional district created by university buildings and the residential neighborhood to the south. The building exterior is clad in a deep orange-colored brick accented by light-colored cast stone that blends in scale and character with adjacent campus buildings, while fenestration of the southern elevation reflects the window type and size of nearby brick town houses.

The eleven story structure, with a floor plate of about 23,000 SF (2,140 SM), is placed on a north-south axis. The 90-foot (27-meter) clear span affords freedom in lab/office space planning, both initially and as research requirements evolve. The client selected a partial racetrack corridor system, internalizing a group of labs in the center for maximum flexibility. This main corridor is exposed to daylight and panoramic views to the east and west, and serves as an excellent interaction space for researchers.

Multipurpose rooms, classrooms, three conference rooms and a large meeting room are located on the first floor adjacent to the main lobby. Functional components, such as elevators, stair towers and ventilator exhausts, provide distinctive architectural elements to define the exterior of the building. The most striking element of the facade is the piano curve that faces west—an organic shape that reflects the biomedical work taking place inside. On each floor, the piano curve harbors interaction lounges that provide opportunity for people to learn from each other through informal encounters.

Recognized by many as "the jewel of the campus," the building houses departments of biochemistry and molecular biology, microbiology and immunology; the Jefferson Institute of Molecular Medicine; the Stein Research Center; and the research division of the departments of dermatology and rheumatology. There are also classrooms, offices, specialty suites and labs.

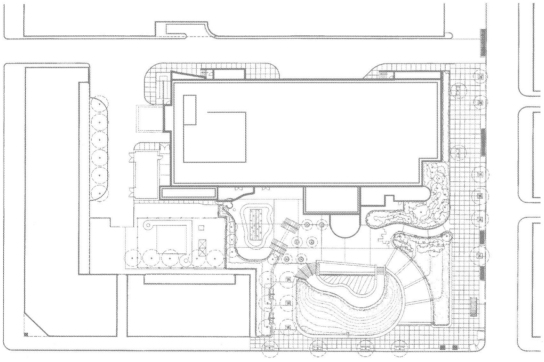

The medical tower is at
the south end of the
one-half block center
city site, providing an
entrance courtyard as a
landscaped haven from
the surrounding noise
and density. Against
the backdrop of the
eleven-story wall, the
entrance element has
been designed to
acknowledge human
scale.

Functional components, such as elevators, stair towers and ventilator exhausts, provide distinctive architectural elements to define the exterior of the building.

Glaxo, Inc.
Pharmaceutical R&D
Headquarters Complex
Research Triangle Park, North Carolina

Glaxo, Inc. initiated their new headquarters project to develop an identifiable, industry- leading research establishment at this Research Triangle site. The facility, designed to strengthen the company's worldwide research objectives, provides complete capabilities for the discovery and development for new drugs in a singular location. The massive complex of labs and offices was planned to present an image consistent with their prominent position in the pharmaceutical industry; housing 2500 scientists and professionals. A fundamental initiative in the design is to foster interrelationship of researchers to increase creativity, productivity and flexibility within a cohesive, humanistic work environment.

The first step of design involved the masterplanning, of 1500 (607 hectares) densely forested and sloping acres, including 2.2 million SF (205,000 SM) of R & D facilities, of which 1.5 million SF (140,000 SM) have been constructed to date. The southernmost portion of the wooded site was developed previously to Kling Lindquist's involvement and was added as support to the Headquarters facility. The existing structures are expansive mid-rise, precast stone, rectilinear buildings; thus setting a vocabulary for the new additions.

The design approach was dominated by a ubiquitous decision to create a visual harmony with the buildings and the existing landscape. To minimize disturbance to land and trees while simultaneously affording the employees a stunning natural setting, the entire complex was planned according to the contours of the North Carolina rolling hills. The "buildings set within the woods" concept also provides point of reference from every vantage. An existing stream was damned to create a series of ponds that enhance the beauty and tranquility of the site. In addition, 3000 new trees and 25,000 shrubs were added to enhance and maintain the environment. Building masses are below the tree line and local materials are extensively used.

Precast walls, detailed to resemble indigenous stone pervade throughout the design. Its dusty rose hue adds coloration, and the banding and differentiation provide human scale. Large windows consistently provide the occupants with view and daylighting; while sunscreens and light reflectors filter the harsh southern sun to create well lighted commodious spaces.

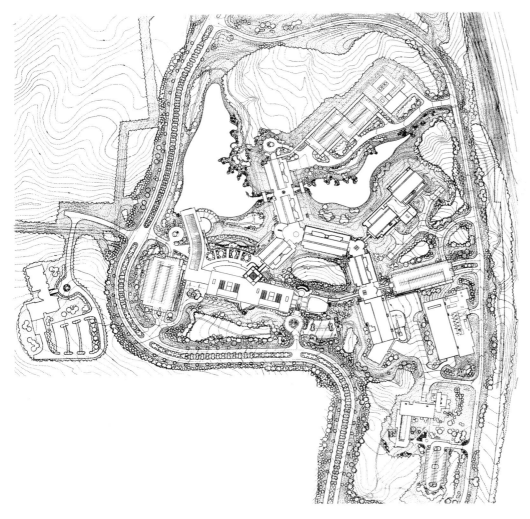

The scale of the overall masterplan meant that opportunities for architectural expression and clarification of movement were both important issues in bringing comfortable scale to the participants.

Circulation patterns and their experiences are critical aspects of the architectural resolution and expression. The employee entrance to the right is linked to the western garage by the arcade shown below.

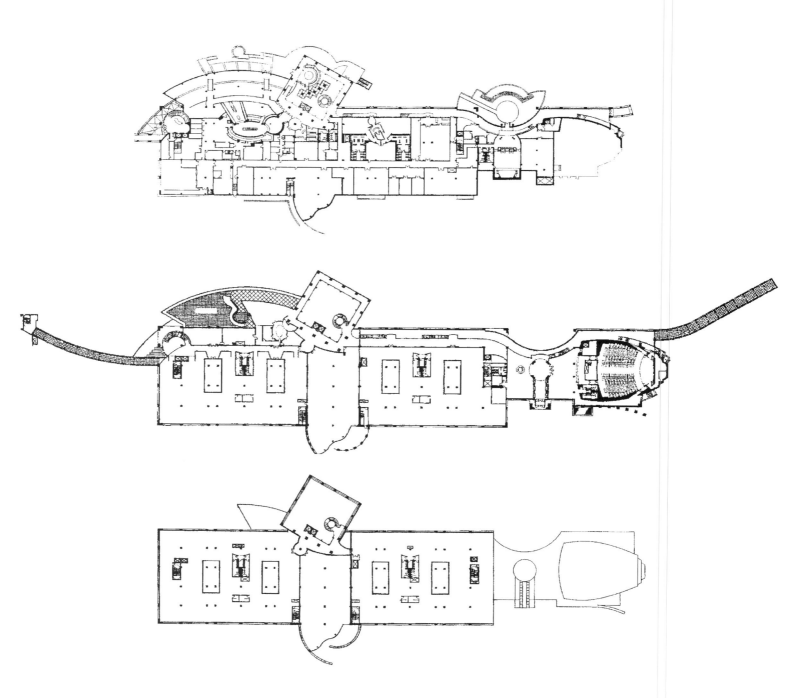

The first floor plan
identifies the main
circulation path which
run along the building's
north face.
This walkway leads
to various destinations:
the auditorium;
executive dining
and cafeteria, left;
and to the office areas
punctuated by small
atria, below.

At night, there is strong indication of the patterns of movement and the grandeur of the shared spaces.

Sterling Winthrop, Inc.
Pharmaceuticals Research Division
R&D Headquarters Complex
Upper Providence Township, Pennsylvania

Located twenty miles west of Philadelphia, Sterling Research Group commissioned Kling Lindquist to design their pharmaceutical headquarters research and development facility. The initial design phase, included a master plan for a 1,500,000 SF (14,000 SM) facility on a 161 acre (65 hectare) rural site. Sloping distinctly to the northeast, the area is copiously occupied by wetlands, one branch of which divides the site into two halves. Due to this constraint, the master plan called for two masses of buildings on opposite sides connected by a tall, linear atrium, which serves to physically and literally conjoin the wet labs and clinical office areas.

Sterling's primary objectives are to create a comfortable environment that fosters interaction, respects nature, and promotes a workplace of high performance. The most challenging litany of requirements sought for a dichotomy in design that presents itself as distinguished, yet not distinctive; one that excels, yet is modest.

The initial increment, completely constructed, is a 910,000 SF (84,650 SM) nine building complex that contains the consolidated administrative headquarters, commons, R & D laboratories and related support areas. The building is organized on a grid, with two primary axes. The east-west spine organizes the research functions, while the north-south spine is a service spine, anchored by the Commons on the north end and the Central Plant at the south.

Furthermore, the facility is organized into four "tiers" of buildings established between major circulation systems. The northernmost tier is designated to non-lab activity for clinical research; the second is wet labs, the third houses drug safety labs, pharmaceutical development labs, and chemical pilot plant; the fourth is the central plant. As a means to shrink the seeming immensity of the complex, the overall plan is organized to give a clear pattern of circulation for people, materials and waste removal. The atrium is the primary reference point where everyone arrives and moves about. To make the visual experience of movement engaging enough to counteract perceived distances, spatial reliefs in the form of courtyards are placed as hinges to hold the various buildings together.

The 40-foot (12.2 M) wide multi-story, naturally lit atrium, terracing down with the natural terrain is divided into three segments. The upper atrium at level 2 serves as the main entrance to the facility. The middle atrium at level 1 is the library, and the lower atrium at the ground level is the cafeteria. Circulation cores, punctuating the atrium at three points, are main connectors to all the levels. These elevator lobbies are design to be major nodes for people of varied disciplines to meet and interact.

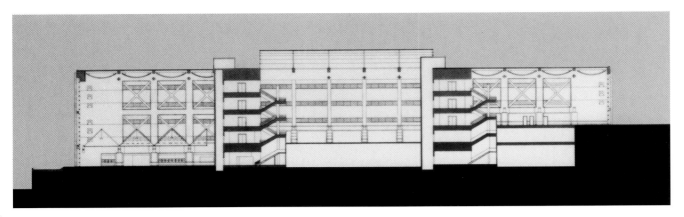

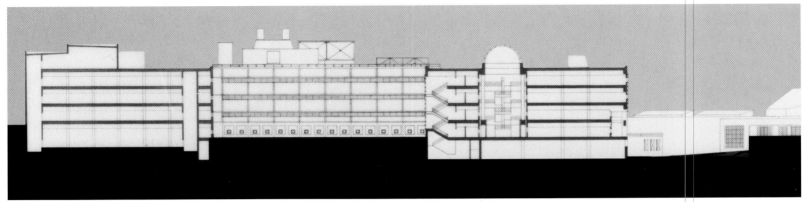

This model evidences the ultimate build out of 1.6 million SF. This magnitude of development is organized around a central linear atrium and is expressed by the structurally expressive bracing on the elevation.

The atrium not only provides orientation upon arrival and clear passage through the complex, but also is activated by program elements including the research library and dining area.

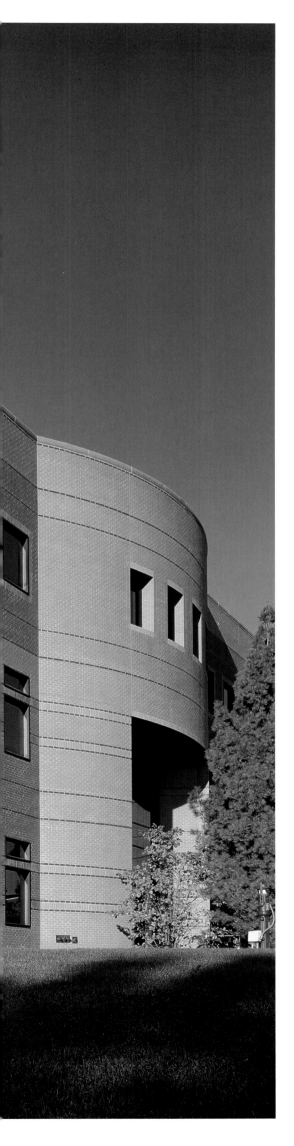

Merck & Co., Inc. Pharmaceutical Research and Development Facility
West Point, Pennsylvania

The Pharmaceutical Research and Development Facility anchors the southeastern edge of the 400 acre Merck campus in a largely corporate, suburban area situated northwest of Philadelphia. Encompassing 218,000-SF, the building marries Pharmaceutical Biophysics, Research, Analysis and Control and Development in a concerted effort by Merck to enhance each division's productivity through the synergy of proximity in a shared support system. The design concept of two discreet, adjacent elements bridged by support areas provides a successful organization to facilitate the transfer of materials and information between the various operations. The three story, masonry structure respectfully acknowledges the existing architecture with both materiality and form. Two parallel wings are linked by a two floor, inset curtainwall block. This configuration allows for a forecourt as a gesture to the campus main entrance gate. The overall design is a direct reflection of the importance of primary adjacencies, while retaining focus of the needs and activities of each scientific unit.

Brick was chosen for the exterior façade to reflect the material vocabulary of the built surroundings. Design features such as punched windows and a series of clerestory windows afford the building anonymity from typical laboratory structures. Hiding the four major roof stacks from pedestrian view through careful placement and elevation design is another solution that lends to its discreet form. Contrasting brick banding wrap the building at its bottom, center and top to reinforce its horizontality. Attentive soldier coursing through rows of punched windows allows the elements to read as a unified feature. An off center protruding full height curvilinear wall reinforces the main entry on the exterior. Upon entry, one will proceed into a triple height, light filled atrium space with a grand stair, revealing the vertical circulation pattern.

The PR&D facility allows for approximately fifty products to be studied or processed independently at any given time. Thus, safety, comfort, efficiency and flexibility evolved as the principal emphases of the building from design inception through completion and utilization. Efficient circulation and distribution patterns are the core factors of the building's layout. The service corridor serves as the central circulation route to accommodate material delivery and maintenance access to utilities. Inter-lab personnel circulation and a second means of egress compose the secondary circulatory paths. The personnel zones are planned to provide a quiet respite from the laboratory environment, with window walls and light filled spaces. This collaboration of design elements allows for a successful flow of multi-tasked and interwoven functions, while facilitating a high quality pharmaceutical research and development environment.

This typical floor plan identifies the differences in the design of spaces and circulation patterns which support research versus development.

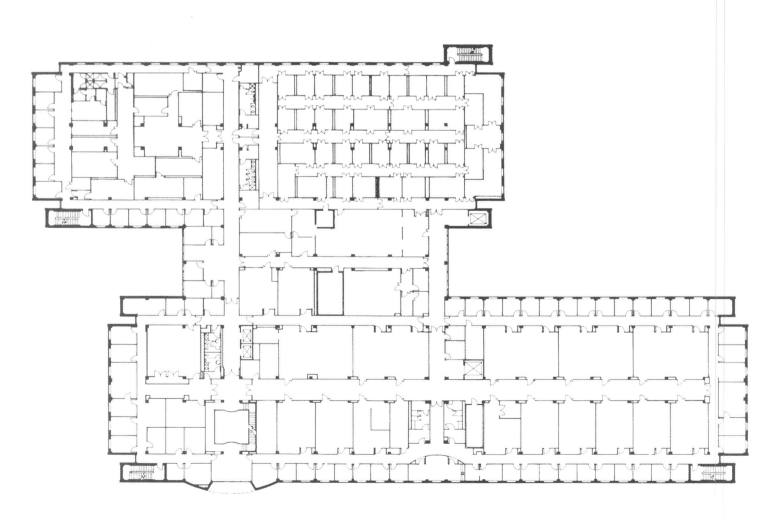

The building is organized as two parallel bars; one primarily focused on research, the other on development. The discreet brick clad masses are offset to create small landscaped courtyards on each side – the character of which is reflected in the wall beyond.

Glaxo Wellcome plc.
Medicines Research Center
Stevenage, Hertfordshire,
United Kingdom

A 163,200 SM (1.8 million SF) state-of-the-art research laboratory and office program on a 30 hectare (73 acre) campus is composed of twelve 4- to 6-story structures, and two 3- and 4-level garages master planned to form a highly interactive campus enhanced by greens, ponds and water features. The objective was to create a quality work environment worthy of world-class scientists and professionals and, at the same time, encourage a close-knit community.

Respect for the semi-rural setting by a project of this size and program required landscaped areas to soften its presence. The main research and administrative buildings are arranged around a central courtyard with the main entrance facing a water meadow developed into a lake. Approached over a pedestrian bridge from the visitor parking area, the 4-story administrative building includes a conference center with a 200-seat lecture theater, seminar room facilities and library; a cafeteria, restaurant; and occupational health and safety functions.

Within the complex, the system of circulation and activities is readily identifiable, providing a logical progression from the entrance and lobby to specialized research areas beyond. Each research building is unique, with differing widths and relationships to windows as appropriate to the functions of the laboratories and offices within.

The multiple research buildings are linked to one another via all-weather, covered pedestrian bridges; each flanked with multi-floor communications nodes composed of stairways, elevators, and informal seating and small conference areas. The 3,000 people of this small "city" are thereby encouraged to encounter and communicate with each other as part of an interactive and productive workplace that promotes interdisciplinary cooperation. Needs for separation and isolation are also provided for specialized laboratories and research areas, while modular lab design is utilized to accommodate layout changes easily and efficiently.

The relatively narrow buildings provide daylight and views for all occupied spaces except where lab activity requires otherwise. Close proximity of buildings required contamination prevention between intakes and exhausts, which had a marked effect on building mass relationships, the facade, and roof profile designs.

Her Majesty the Queen of England, officially opened the complex on April 19, 1995.

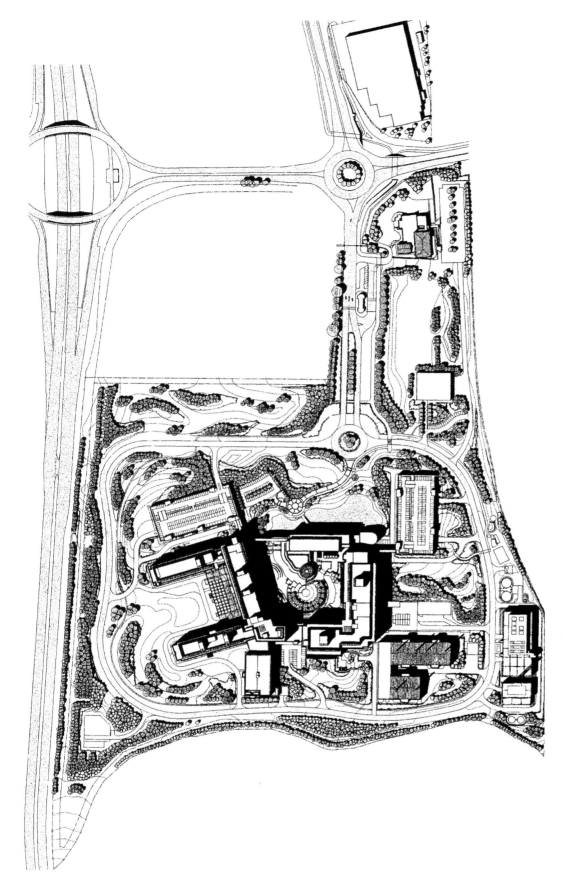

The site plan evidences the care with which the landscape was combined with the architecture to create a setting focused on softening the scientific environment. Three laboratory wings share the courtyard; the pond is an element of the formal arrival sequence.

The courtyard provides a highly designed central focus shared by both researchers and administrators.

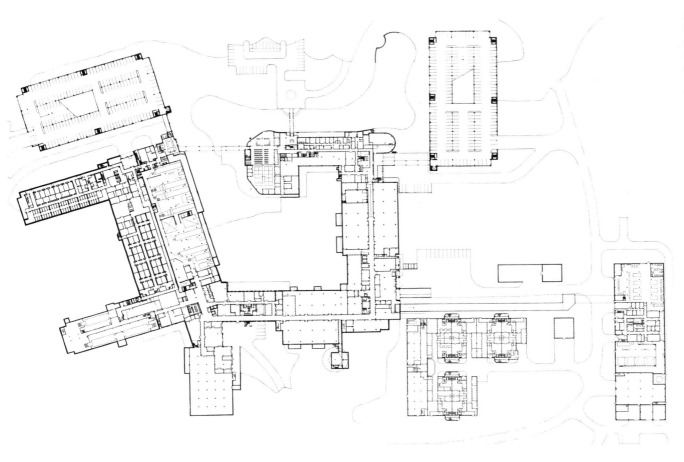

Each scientific discipline has had laboratories specifically created to optimize their process of discovery. The provision of daylight to those spaces, however, is a constant.

QVC
Corporate and Broadcasting Facility
West Goshen, Pennsylvania

In response to a design competition to address the needs of the rapidly evolving electronic retail industry, QVC required a new corporate headquarters that would embrace a diverse set of interrelated functions. They had acquired a 20 year old, light industrial facility to be transformed into offices, production studios, a warehouse and a host of operations and staff related support functions. The heart of this operation would be the TV studio as the platform from which QVC markets its wares.

The program of 555,000 SF (52,000 SM) entailed 50 percent offices (including expansion), 20 percent special/support spaces, and 30 percent warehouse. Each macro and micro program element has unique design requirements for which establishing a highly functional and exciting "QVC Village" was essential. Internal and external environment, image and design quality must establish a gracious setting to accommodate staff, visitors and celebrities.

Kling Lindquist chose to explore realms beyond probability with overt responses that would transform this utterly mundane building into something dramatic and special. In one design we tore off the roof and replaced with multiple conic, billowing tent-like roofs.

In another design, we replaced walls with glass, lacerating them with perpendicular glass walls that extend out into the semi-rural environment.

A third design created a fantasy interior outfitted with a jungle-gym-like super structure.

Finally, a fourth design subdivided the interior environment along the lines of urban planning, complete with streets, private residences, public squares, a town hall, etc.

These explorations led to a dynamically energized design in which production crews can successfully and efficiently do their work both behind the scenes and on-stage. Meanwhile, the dual issues of handling concerns of the privacy and comfort of celebrities while accommodating public tours are managed with ease.

The first plan is organized by clear glass walls which transverse the office environment. The four elevations present different differing architectural approaches including: enveloping the building with a steel grid and pavilions, teflon fabric tents providing the office space with daylight, planar glass walls bisecting the office plan and extending into the landscape (as shown at right), a more conventional approach of redefining the existing enclosure with a sophisticated curtain wall.

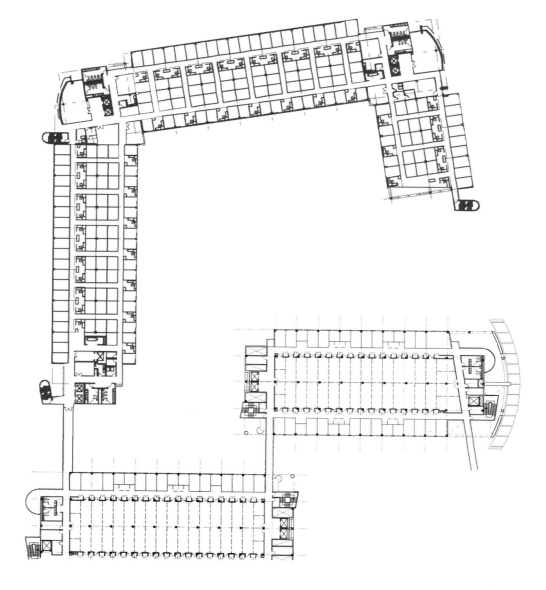

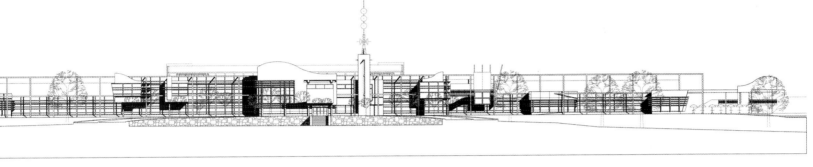
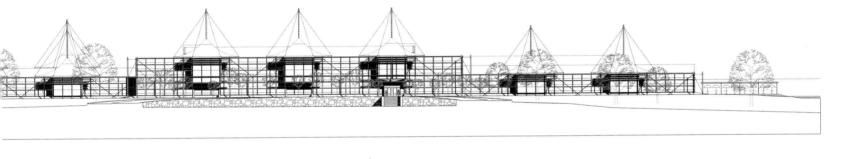
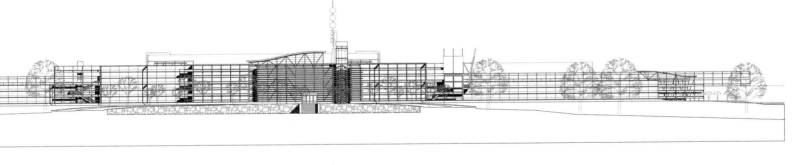
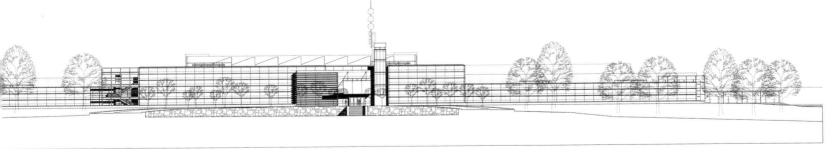

The competition explored varying office designs, and the character of the congregation and nodal spaces. The rotunda was envisioned as the primary public destination. Consistent in the explorations was public arrival, which manifested QVC's activities, and the television studios to which visitors could be invited.

The QVC new corporate
and broadcasting
facility is conceived
as a hight functional
operations village.

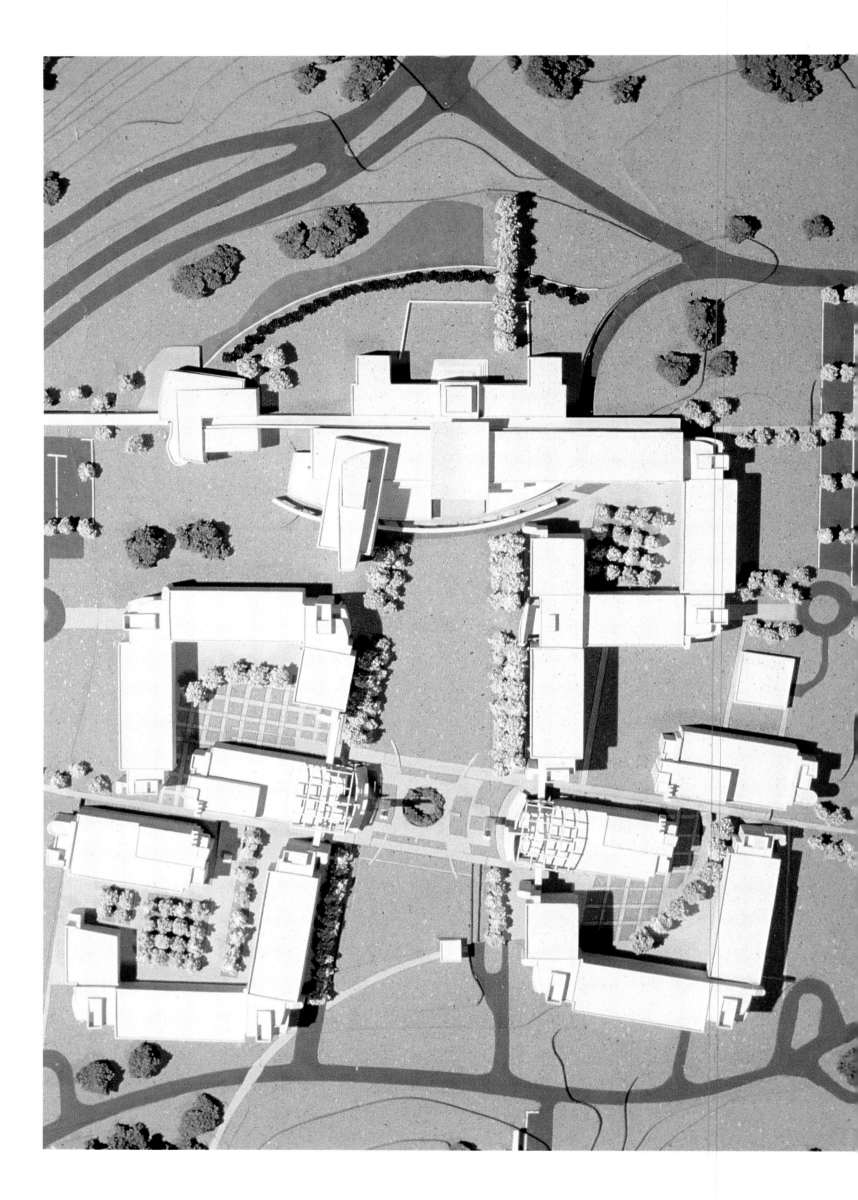

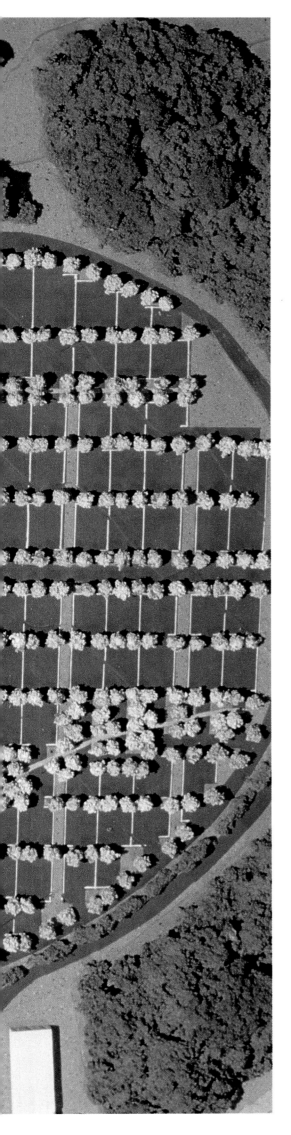

United States Food and Drug Administration Headquarters Consolidation
White Oak, Maryland

The FDA, housed in more than 40 buildings at 18 different locations in the Washington, DC, region, needed to consolidate and streamline its many functions which has resulted in the design of a phased 2.1 million SF (195,300 SM) headquarters and laboratory campus. The project's major objectives were:

• Consolidate the FDA Headquarters (Offices of the Commissioner and of Regulatory Affairs) and three Centers: Drug Evaluation and Research (CDER), Devices and Radiological Health (CDRH) and Biologic Evaluation and Research (CBER) into a single campus to improve operating efficiencies.

• Develop state-of-the-art laboratories and offices flexible enough to adapt to changes required by the FDA in the future.

The project calls for sensitive reuse of the Naval Laboratory Campus at White Oak, Maryland. GSA took ownership of the entire site in 1997 and is managing the development process for FDA, which is to be built in five or six phases over a period of eight to ten years. The FDA will utilize 130 acres (53 hectares) of the campus, maintain existing community facilities, and preserve environmentally sensitive site areas.

The program responds to agency structure and mission changes studied by the US Congress and the FDA, and also recognizes a major shift in the organization from laboratory to office-based work. The programming team developed a common lab building and module, which, in ninety percent of the laboratories, will allow the identified design standards to provide maximal flexibility for varied utilization of the spaces. The team similarly developed a generic office building design that can be expanded or contracted according to needs. It utilizes central nodes from which multiple wings can be built, providing flexibility for office space development and use. Consolidation will afford reduced commons facility requirements.

The Master Plan for the entire campus includes reuse and modernization of some landmark facilities. Masonry sympathetic to the retained buildings is envisioned as the primary material for the office buildings; while the laboratories are planned to be clad in metal panels with expressed mechanical elements to more clearly identify their scientific purpose.

The FDA campus is organized around a grand central lawn, which serves as the shared focal point. Courtyards defined by a combination of research laboratories and administrative offices give a singular home to each of the centers.

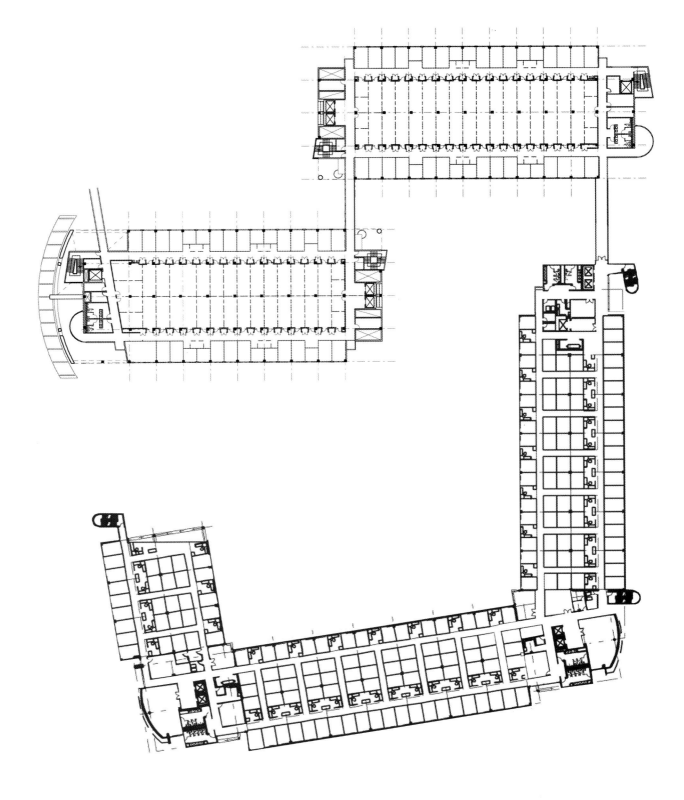

Glaxo France Administrative Headquarters Campus
Marly-le-Roy, France

Located on a historically and environmentally sensitive site near Versailles, this headquarters design was predicated on phased growth which would be respectful of both the area's traditions and the prevalent residential scale of its neighbors. Foremost in the design's resolution was consideration of the buildings' integration with the site's continuously sloped surface.

Programmatically the complex was envisioned as being constructed in three phases of 27,000 SM, 6500 SM, and 10,500 SM, with a population which would ultimately double from its first occupancy of 450. In support of the office environment have been planned food service facilities, training areas, a fitness club, and a 300 seat auditorium which has been physically separated in order to allow it to be shared with the local community. Parking and service areas are placed beneath the buildings to minimize their visibility.

The first phase design is composed of five "L" shaped office elements defining four intermediary courtyards. The 16m wide buildings are intended to accommodate both private offices and open workstations, with their commonality being consideration for maximizing daylight and natural ventilation. Each of the courtyards has been designed both to be viewed and to be experienced; and each has taken a different aspect of French landscape tradition as its premise.

The buildings are clad in locally quarried limestone and are articulated with aluminum fins and light shelves. Expansive areas of clear glass further define the office blocks; and clear glass towers identify the vertical circulation nodes along the north facade.

Retained apple orchards and expansive lawns are complemented by manmade watercourses and areas of formal planting. Both the buildings and the landscape work together to reflect the humanistic and historical values shared by Glaxo and the town of Marly-le-Roi.

The north wall of the complex is punctuated by vertical circulation towers, which mediate the sloped terrain. Between these elements, differing programmatic functions extend into the landscape.

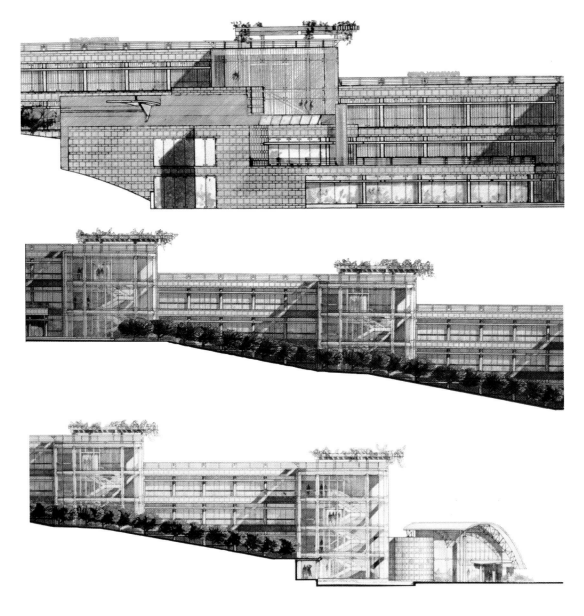

The revised project consists of three, instead of five, wings with wider resulting courts between. Columns, sunscreens and terraces modulate French limestone walls.

City of Shenzhen Television Center
Shenzhen, China

The city of Shenzhen is positioned like a hinge at the frontier of two economic systems and ideological societies: Hong Kong and Mainland China. Physical development of this new city has attracted international attention as an arena for uncovering new and/or renewed paradigms of urbanism and architecture.

In less than 20 years, Shenzhen has grown from a fishing village of 15,000 people into a metropolis with a population of three million (four, including the "floating mass"), placing it at the forefront of the global stage. The center of the city, originally planned for one million people, has been enlarged and relocated, forming the Futian New City Center. As a highly focused and publicized urban event, the infrastructure of the new city center was planned and implemented by 1995, taking less than three years. Since then, major public facilities have been planned and financed by the city government to materialize its "blueprinted" visions.

The Shenzhen TV Station is the first public building located in the Futian New City Center. Playing the leading role of Futian's new architecture, this project intends to manifest new aesthetics of speed, efficiency, mass media, and futuristic goals of the society. The 45,000 SM (485,000 SF) building's program includes one theater-type studio of 1,000 seats, four medium-sized studios, a number of small news studios; program production facilities, headquarters offices and a large public congregation space. The planning ordinance designated a plot ratio of 2.24, site coverage of 34 percent, and height limit of 100 meters (394 feet).

This proposal establishes a clear stratification from the south to the north and ranges from the public plaza, public congregation hall and public service/entrance to the studios and production service areas. The design responds to site circulation conditions while fulfilling the specific procedures of broadcasting. Revealing studio production activities to the congregation area brings monumentality to the public space while fully expressing the essence of mass media.

The elliptical mass of the theater studio penetrates through the congregation hall into the public plaza to function as a ceremonial urban theater inside and as public art outside. The headquarters office tower broadcasts news at its top via LED across the skyline of the city to the surrounding hilly horizons . Positioned at the west edge of the site, which is located at the western edge of the Futian New City Center, the tower serves as a threshold of the new Futian district. The nature of the design, which begins "void" on the south and progresses to "solid" on the north, honors Feng Shui, an awareness of energy flow in the built environment that prevails in this area of China.

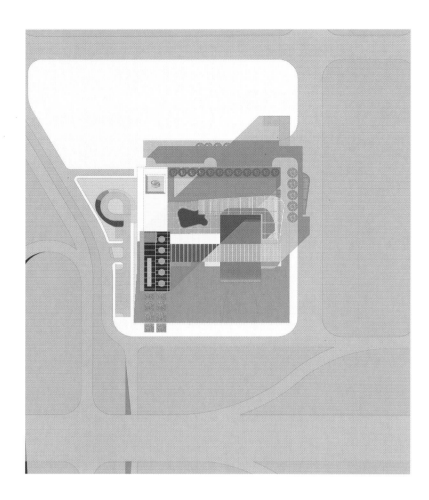

The site plan reflects the sense of containment, which the tower and studio bar bring to the site. The plans and section identify the layering of public and private spaces as one moves onto the site from the south.

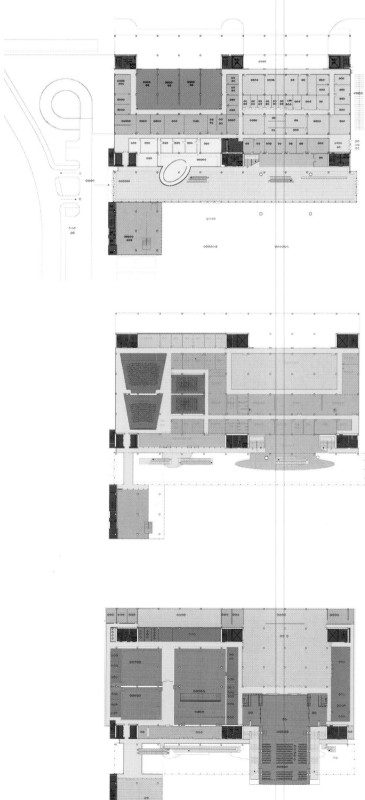

The atrium and projecting broadcast studio are both the primary public realms and the symbol for the television station. To the west, the tower presents a planar but shifted stainless steel wall and a large window as a beacon.

City of Shenzhen Cultural Center
Shenzhen, China

The Futian New City Center in the rapidly developing city of Shenzhen, China, poised between the contrasting economic and cultural worlds of Hong Kong and the Mainland, is based on classical planning principles. A grand north-south central axis from the hills to the bay, Shenzhen planners recognized, must be supported by a series of public facilities among which there is a heart. Thus the Shenzhen Cultural Center project was born. Comprising the New City Hall, the Youth Palace and the Cultural Center, City Hall is situated on the axis, while the Youth Palace and Cultural Center face each other across the axis just south of City Hall.

The Shenzhen Cultural Center includes: the 35,000 SM (375,000 SF) Shenzhen Central Library with a book collection of 4,000,000 volumes; a music hall with 2000 seats and a 6,000 SM (64,500 SF) musical museum; a large conference hall for city-wide public events; areas for a series of commercial and entertainment functions.

The overall site area is 55,846 SM (600,000 SF). The planning ordinance designates a plot ratio of 0.8 for the music hall and 1.2 for the library; site coverage of 55 percent and height limit of 60 meters (197 feet).

The proposed project uses the natural force of the landscape as a strategy to establish a hierarchy among program components and spatial sequences. A territorially scaled sloped plane separates the street-oriented, "profane" programs below: automobile traffic, Southern China street life, service, commercial and entertainment functions, from the "sacred" activities above: a monumental plaza and the ascending monuments of Shenzhen's new identity.

The library rises above the sloped plane at the south end at the start of the slope. It forms a "flying courtyard" above a large artificial water pond—the most traditional form of Chinese secular building that signifies the highest tranquility and transcending intellectuality in modern urban life.

Two volumes compose the music hall: one solid that encompasses the performance areas and requisite acoustics, the other a void to accommodate public interactions before and after performances. The solid volume is imbedded in the open one, which is treated as a glass shaft cutting through the sloped plane. It provides all vertical circulation spaces and two levels of public entry: on the street and on the plaza. The solid volume is sculpted from both inside and out to support the acoustics for the types of music and performance within, while honoring the Eastern notion of monumentality on the outside, which is represented by the roof and its relation to the sky. The outer surface is designed to both achieve and challenge monumentality by confusing the differentiation between roof and wall. Its continuous concave and convex surface engages with the sky and mountains in the background. Inner and outer surfaces create cavities for service shafts, fire egresses and extra noise barriers.

Acoustics are a major challenge for the multipurpose and multicultural hall. Performances can range from symphonic orchestra to chamber music, from Chinese drama to Southeast Asian music ensembles and Indian performance. The acoustic environment must vary from standard orchestra requirements to a quasi-outdoor atmosphere. The hall, therefore, has a computerized, removable ceiling above which is a reverberance chamber. As the ceiling is removed, in whole or in part, the hall is reconfigured to rooms appropriate for different audience sizes and reverberation times. It's an acoustic chameleon.

The conceptual watercolor studies were the earliest exploration of public environments. In the approach to the siting, and plan and section resolution, the issues relating to large-scale congregation are most critical.

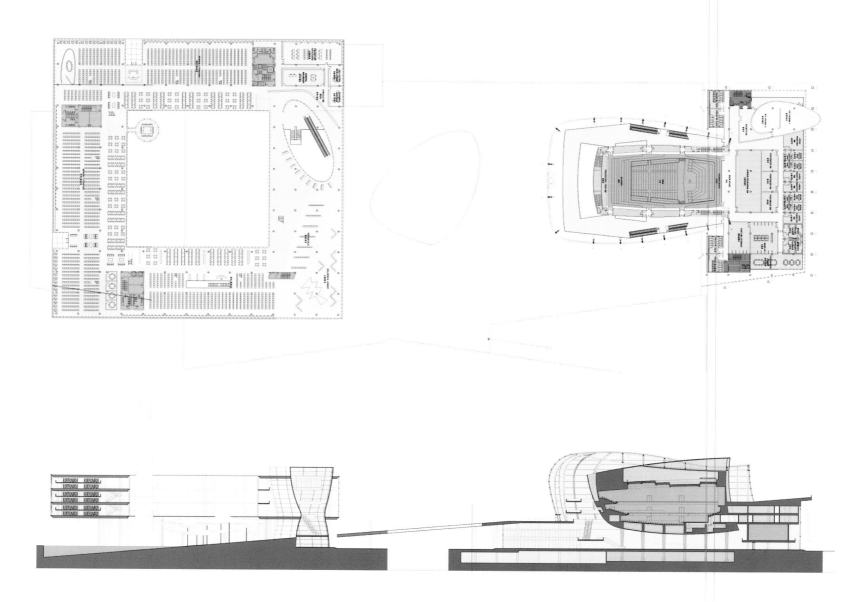

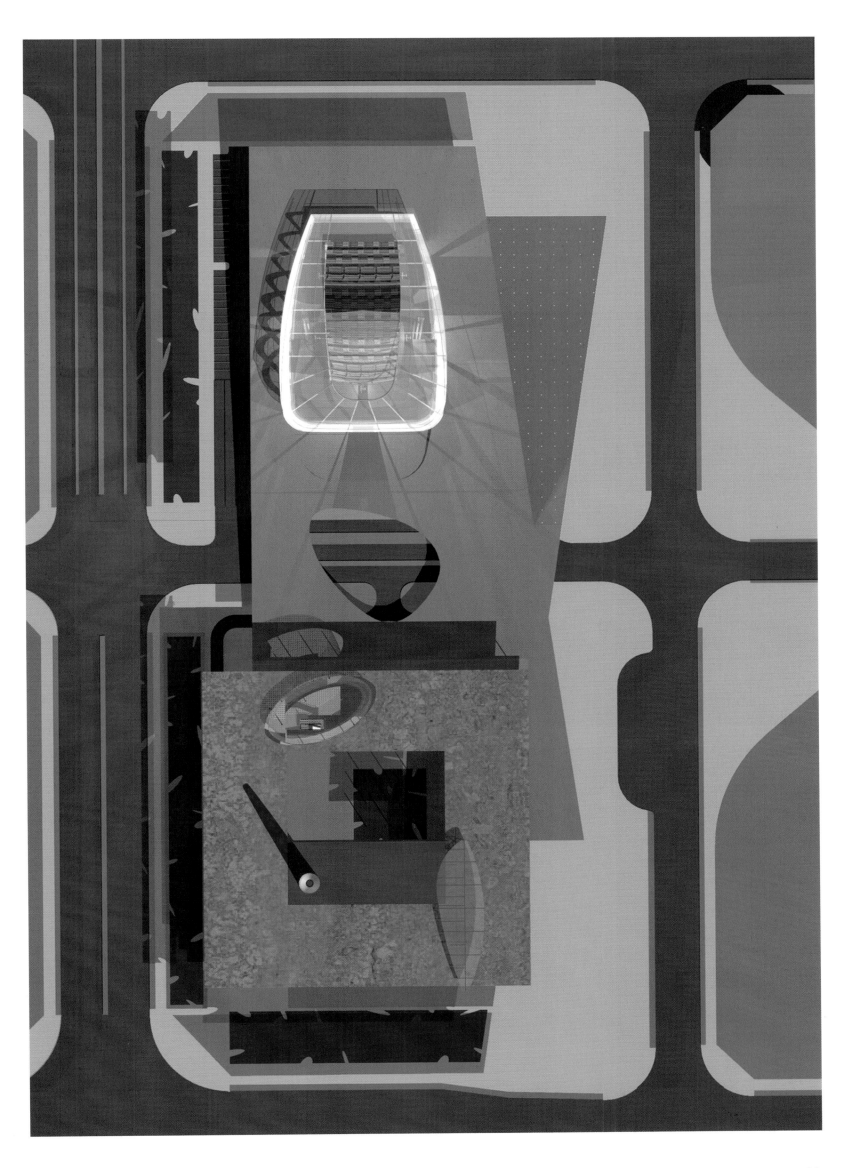

As evidenced by both
the model photographs
and elevation, the
sloped plane transitions
from being ground to
roof, while is suggests a
link between the
cultural center and the
ceremonial hill to the
north.

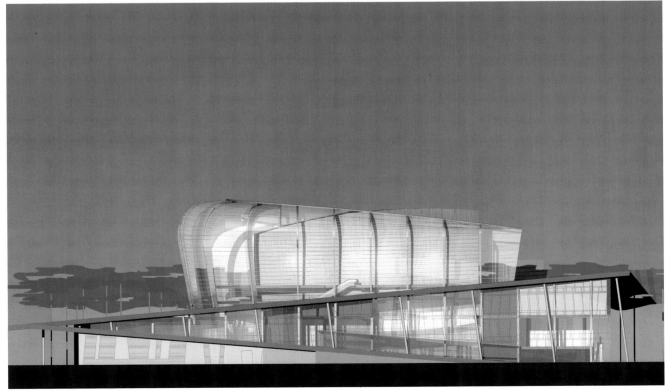

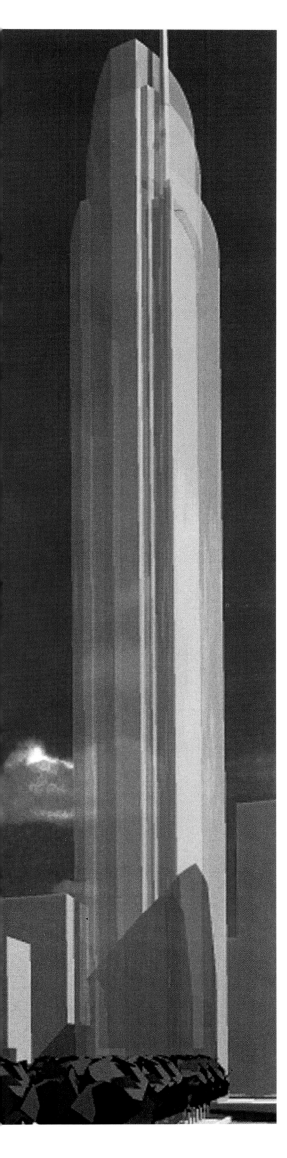

Center City Office Tower
Philadelphia, Pennsylvania

One of Philadelphia's most important urban addresses was made available as a result of a fire, which caused significant damage to a 1970's vintage high-rise. The site is directly opposite City Hall, and defined by a context of buildings which have existed for thirty years or longer. It is within these conditions, and with regard to the historical importance of the city's center, that these studies were executed.

The primary candidate is a softly curved seventy-story tower. Intentionally designed to manifest an identity without direct reference to the site's history, the building is placed to mitigate the restrictive physical conditions which restrict this particular city block - as both pedestrian level experience, and as an aspect of the city's skyline.

At Grade A plaza and reflecting pool allow enhanced visual access south along Fifteenth Street; and, more importantly, bring the City Hall's Dillworth Plaza into a continuum of the urban fabric. At its apex the tower gradually evolves into a form separate from, but respectful of, the Beaux-Arts spire which culminates the city government's home.

The total area of 1.4 million SF (130,000 SM) is comprised of typical floor plans of 25,000 SF, but these reduce to 8,000 SF at the top. Proposed below grade parking for 200 cars is accomplished without compromise to the very important underground concourse which ties the city's buildings and transportation links together.

Clad in clear and silk-screened vision glass, the design intent is to create a highly identifiable translucent object as a dominant, but self-effacing, element of this city's skyline. An element which even while passing from transparency to reflectivity continuously acts as a beacon celebrating Philadelphia's future.

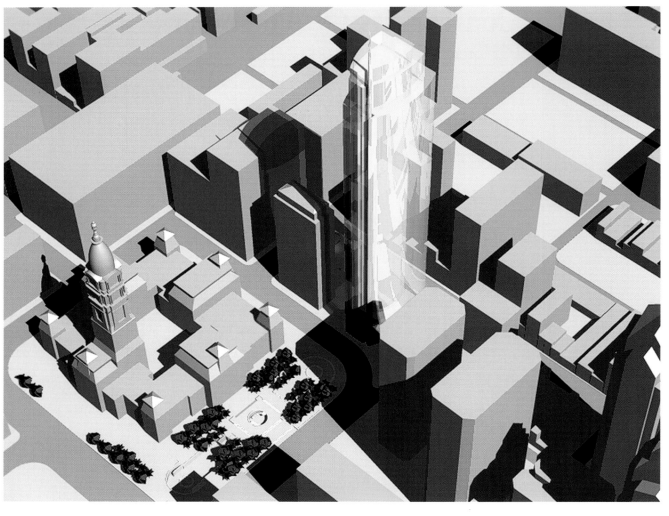

The tower's placement terminates the axis created by City Hall's west plaza and establishes a more gracious pedestrian environment.

Dow Jones & Co., Inc. Corporate Office Facility
Princeton, New Jersey

The design was determined during an invited competition composed of a master plan focusing on the addition of 900,000SF; a first phase corporate office facility of 450,000GSF and parking for 1200 cars. Significant issues of resolution included incorporation of the new large structure within a campus without benefit of a plan for growth; and the requirement that this facility link the four existing structures which had neither a commonality of orientation nor scale.

The building is sited with the intention of creating a more cohesive campus; while endeavoring to present with the rotunda, a clear destination to people arriving from Route 1. The bridge across the main entry drive linking to the three easterly buildings, and the on-grade connection to the information services building provide sheltered access to the primary elements of the campus. The internal organization of the new facility responds to the issue of pedestrian traffic with a 700-foot long grand avenue running along the long axis.

The skylit atrium not only infuses the office environment with natural light, but also continues the clear pattern of circulation established on the first floor. Primary corridors along the atrium edges connect four discrete cores and the four primary communication stairways.

The architectural character has been determined in direct response to the existing context. Careful orchestration of massing components: parallel planes, volumes defined by seemingly discrete walls, a tripartite organization of the main office block, and the layering of forms - all endeavor to balance the new building's scale with the present very large and very small structures.

The Indiana limestone cladding was chosen for its responsiveness to the single existing limestone and the three existing precast-faced structures. The stone's coloration harmonizes with the various beige tonalities, while its variegation further addresses the issue of scale. Clear glass windows are enhanced by a low E coating, and are defined by custom extruded painted aluminum framing.

A landscaped courtyard has been designed between the two main buildings. Anchored by a central round garden of bamboo, enameled stones, and rock formations; this courtyard is planned to accommodate exterior dining and provide a place of respite for people from both facilities. Landscaping and curvilinear walls and walkways integrate the new area with both the new building and the present campus.

Issues inherent to the creation of an optimal open office environment - daylight, indirect lighting, efficiency and flexibility, primarily condition the interior organization. Open workstations, which accommodate 90% of the population, were a significant determiner of column grids and circulation patterns. A fourth floor executive area, floor by floor conferencing and employee amenity facilities, and sophisticated communication support rooms are other aspects of the office zone. The more public realm of this facility is primarily relegated to first and basement floors, and includes a fitness center, company store and café, and a gallery which is intended for changing exhibitions as well as for display of company artifacts.

The atrium is clad in green serpentine paving and will soon be softened by bamboo. Cantilevered glass railings above, and clear glass walls at the first floor describe its edges. The "wishbone" tracery which supports the skylight has been designed to not only glorify the space, but also resolve seismic force requirements to tie the building halves together.

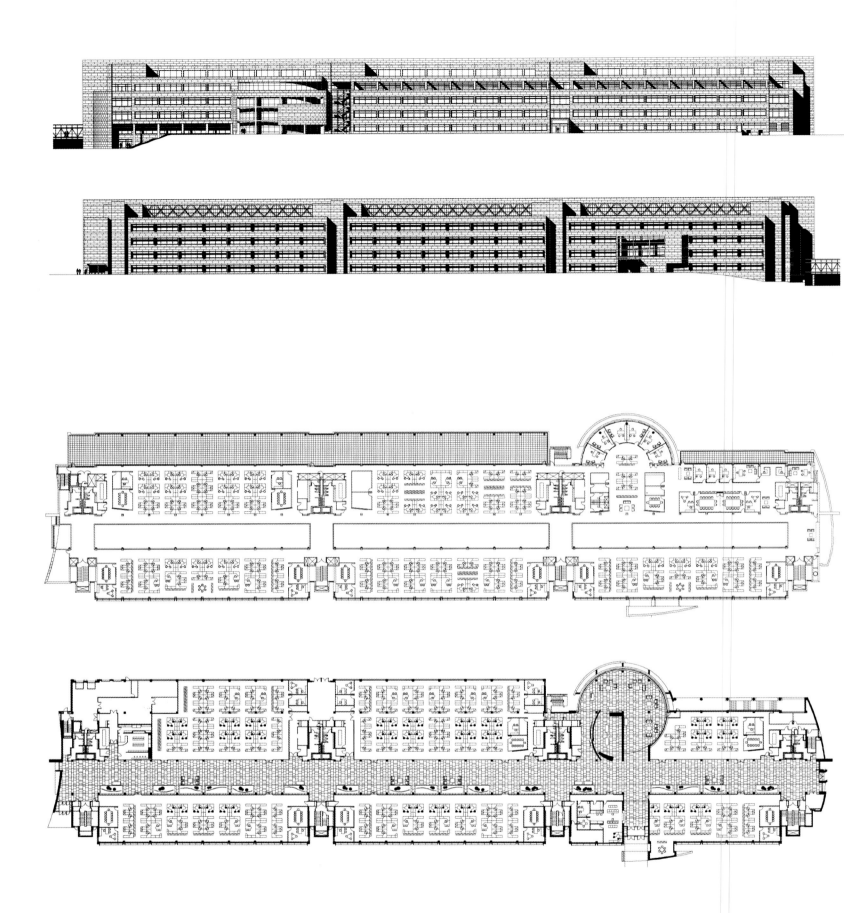

The elevations and
photographs speak to
the highly layered
character of the
facades. The plans
indicate the very open
office environment,
which takes full
advantage of the
provided daylight.

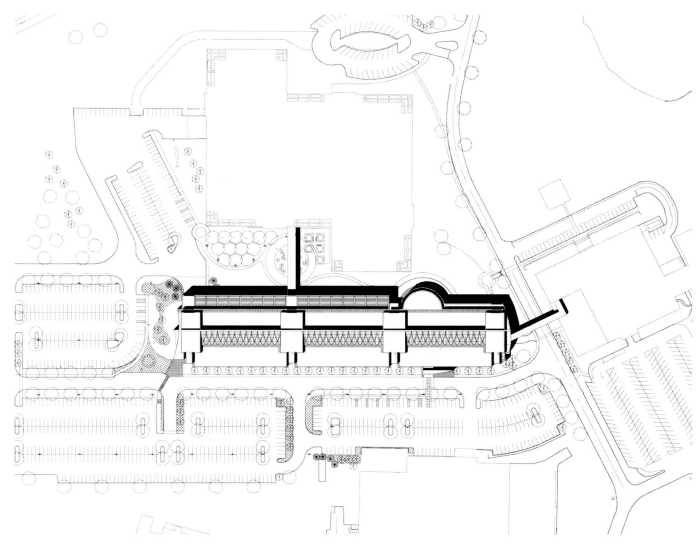

Extended walls, sunscreens, and layered patterns of aluminum coupled with the variegated and differentiated stone provide human scale to the large structure.

The atrium is the primary organizer of the space, and is enhanced by the almost gothic tracery of the skylight structure.

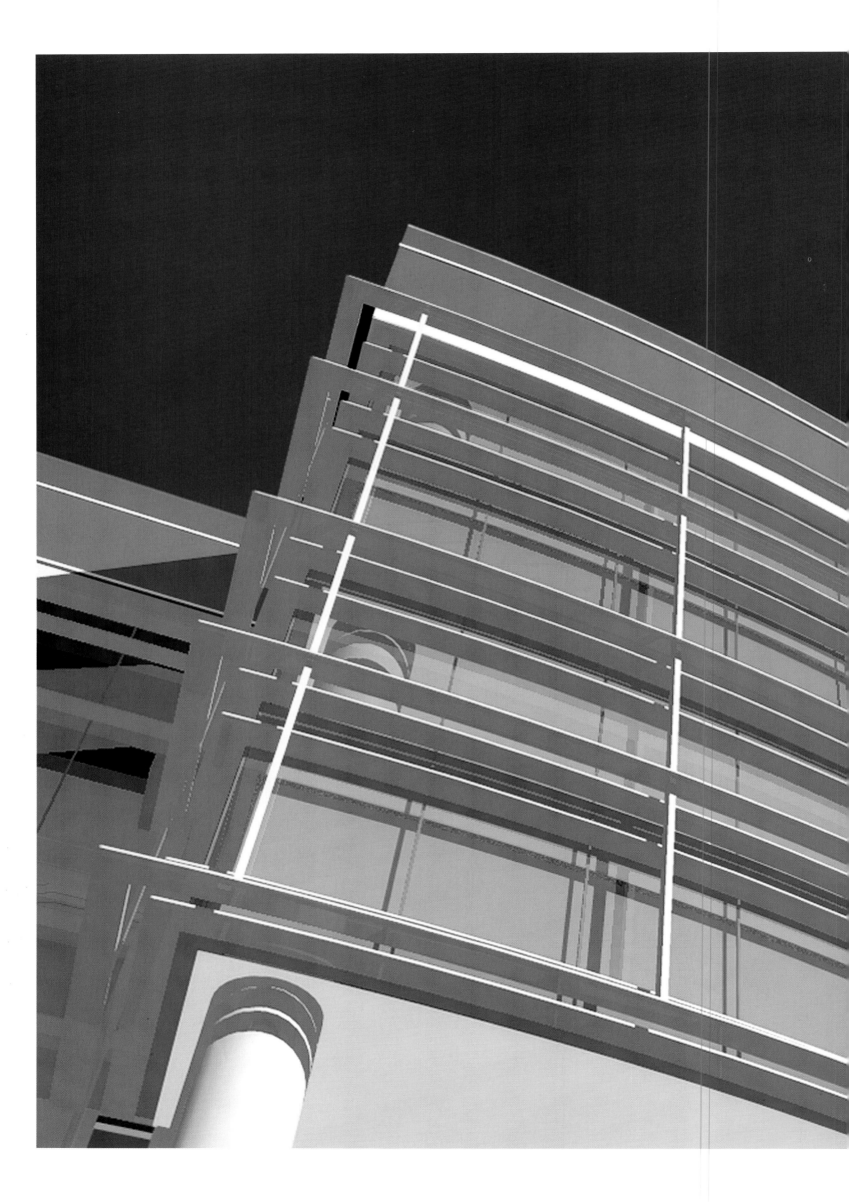

Merck & Co., Inc.
Multi-Science Facility
Rahway, New Jersey

Merck's most advanced laboratory facility has been designed to accommodate the requirements of process chemistry, combinatorial synthesis, and medicinal chemistry research. Sophisticated laboratories, lab support spaces, scientist and administrative offices, and congregation areas have been carefully orchestrated to promote collaboration and discovery within an environment which used as its primary basis of design, the provision of safety.

The new facilities are designed to be consistent with the Rahway campus with respect to building material, color, and scale; allowing the building, together with extensive site and landscape design improvements, to make a significant contribution to both the semi-industrial site and the neighboring residential areas. Patterned brick, limestone banding, and highly profiled aluminum framing are composed to accentuate the horizontality of the 700 foot (213 meter) long structure along its north and south faces. In a similar spirit of integration, design of the narrow end elevations draws the metal panels from the penthouse into the body of the building, thereby presenting a highly layered composition appropriate to the scale of the neighboring buildings.

To the north the building addresses the primary pedestrian zone within the campus, and presents to this environment discrete curvalinear entrance placards, and break rooms identifiable as projected parallel planes. Arced paths and small paved forecourts tie the facility to preexisting campus circulation patterns. To the south, across a landscaped courtyard, the facility is linked to a 680 space parking garage, designed to be sympathetic to the research building's character.

These considerations of environment are more than balanced by considerations contributing to scientific discovery: synthesis labs, NMR's, accommodation of robotics and analytical instrumentation, and wide ranging portable equipment reinforce the diverse research approach. Other unique support spaces are provided for developing new automation methodologies and screening and assay of chemical compounds. Within the 322,000 SF (30,000 SM) structure the systems, equipment, and environment exist for a flexible approach to drug discovery which will readily adapt over time.

Each articulation is not only expressive of an internal programmatic resolution, but contributory to a campus which is as much about building edges.

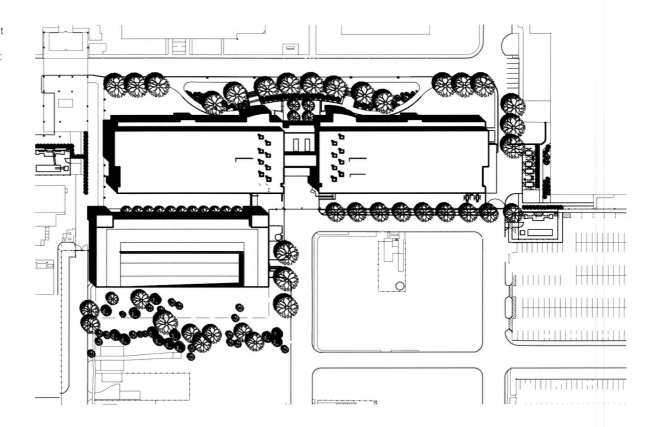

The typical laboratory
floor plans represent a
clarity of both people
and service circulation,
and laboratories which
reflect variable sized
team approaches.

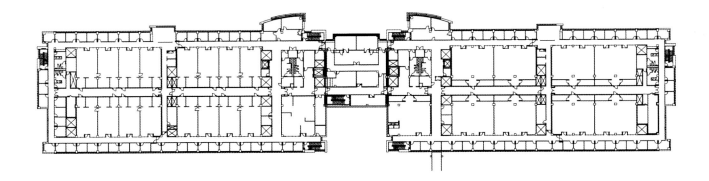

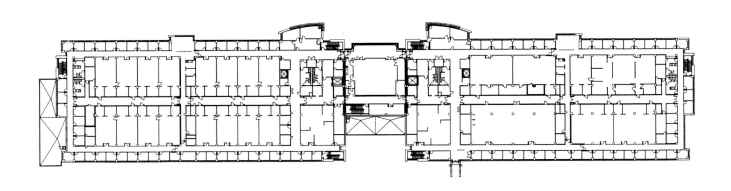

Exterior wall designs explored stone and metal lintels, decorative brick patterns, soldier courses, and varying degrees of striation. The photographs of the almost complete enclosure indicate the chosen design direction.

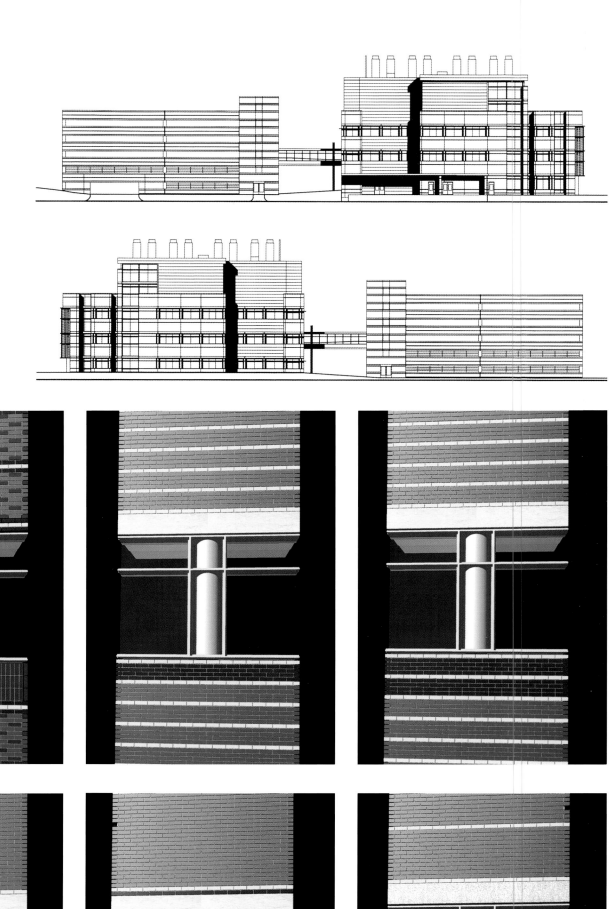

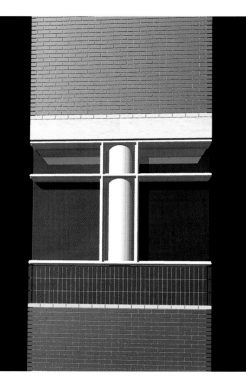

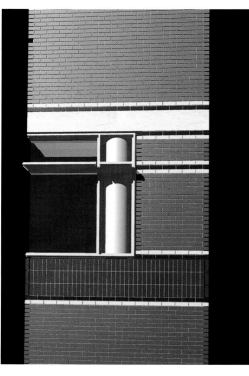

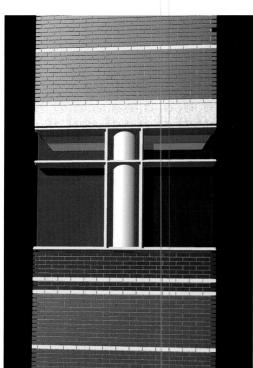

SAP America, Inc. Corporate Headquarters
Newtown Square, Pennsylvania

Located in a semi-rural suburb of Philadelphia, the 400,000 SF (37,200 SM) building accommodates 1,200 employees and up to 600 visitors to the demonstration and training centers which fulfill important functions for the company's products and services. The master plan includes a Phase II building of similar size and extension of the 1,000-car parking structure.

The building's role as a corporate headquarters demanded that the project present a distinctive image, while its location motivated sensitivity to the farmland scale of the landscape and the small-town scale of its nearest neighboring buildings. The master planning requirements, and the presence of precious trees on the nearly pristine site, presented a paradoxical matrix of conditions. Sited on the brow of a hill along a serpentine entry road, the building height yields to surrounding trees. The predominantly south-facing exterior wall of the 1,000-foot long (305-meter) structure parallels a preexisting access road and curves so that the east end parallels nearby buildings. The structured parking facility is placed in a natural low area parallel to the eastern portion of the elegant arc of the northern side, which also harbors a glass-roofed entrance lobby and a large courtyard. The transparent exterior of green tinted glass reflects and/or dissolves this highly geometric form into the texture, colors and seasonal changes of the surrounding landscape.

The glass enclosed entrance lobby, shared by employees and visitors alike, provides a clear orientation to the building's three main elements of traffic: controlled passage of employees to the office areas, trainees to training areas on the second floor and prospective clients to the third floor. The large auditorium on the first floor (sloped into the basement level) is the hub of activity where all of the building's users may intersect.

A 1,000-foot long, 20-foot wide uninterrupted atrium along the north wall is the main street of the building. Open to each floor, it provides views of the landscaped courtyard and trees beyond through a 45-foot high clear glass wall facing north. The atrium connects the spaces of the three main office floors and serves as the circulation link to the entrance lobby, auditorium, conference rooms and amenity areas such as convenience stores and services and a fitness center.

The relatively narrow floor plate (87 feet from north to south) and its open configuration maximizes natural light into the interior and preserves views to the outside from the vast majority of work areas. No program element touches an outside wall due to corridors along both the south wall and atrium edge. The narrowing of the building to a point at the west end, location of the fitness center and special conference areas, affords exceptional views of the surrounding landscape.

The building has two wall systems: the aforementioned glass wall at the atrium predominantly to the north, and a floor-to-ceiling curtain wall of blue-green glass predominantly to the south. In addition to allowing light and views into the building, the glass surfaces exploit the specific qualities of the material for the building's image within the landscape.

Every effort is being made to maintain mature plantings and natural contours of the land to create a sense of continuum with the nationally registered arboretum. Entrance to the building is via a formal, granite-edged drive through a "great lawn" with a drop-off area alongside a center sculptural fountain. The open lawn area permits unobstructed views to a the myriad of unique tree species, while landscaped areas near the buildings provide softening plantings and paved terraces.

The design for the American Headquarters of the European based computer software company is predicated on the dual issues of identity and respect for the environment. The building is to be expressive of technology characters ascribed to and the dynamics of its workforce. The primary intended image is that of an "antfarm" – a clear enclosure within which there is relentless activity.

The building's curvature allows awareness of one's relationship to the other areas from within the building. With the execution of the second phase, the courtyard will be clearly defined as the heart of the complex.

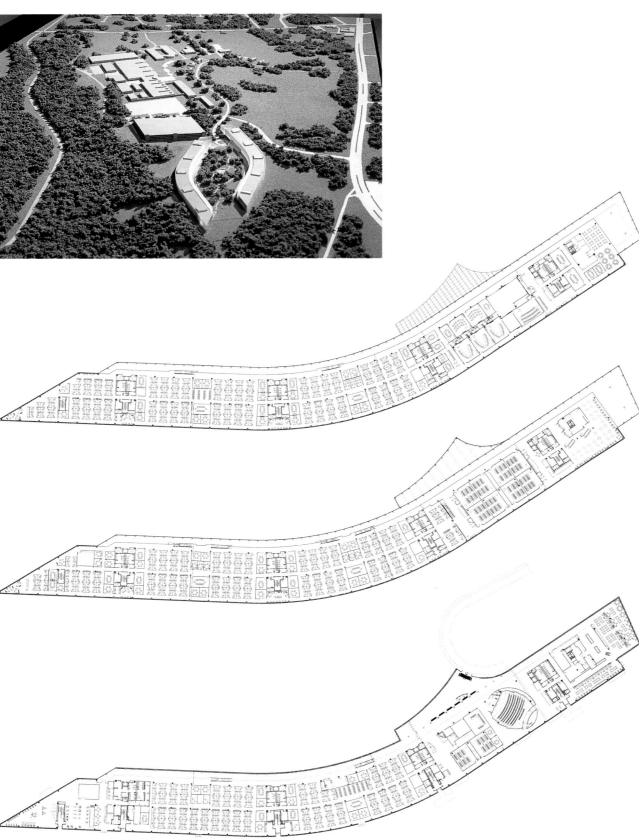

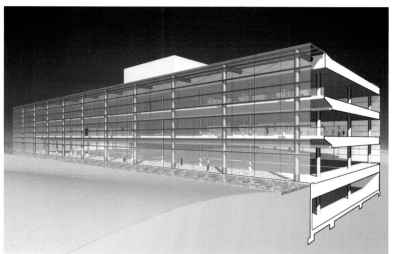

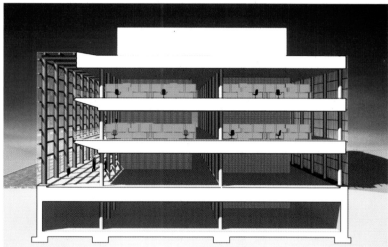

The north wall's transparency was the generative idea behind the design.

The atrium grants abundant daylight to the offices, clarifies movement, and addresses the issue of expressing technology as the basis of SAP's identity.

Kling Lindquist Retrospective

Kling Lindquist's evolution has been a gradual and multifaceted process over the fifty-three years of our history. From Vincent Kling's establishment of his firm as a sole proprietorship in 1946, to today's broadly based leadership, the constant has been to build with respect for the environment. From a practice founded solely within the domain of architecture, to the present team of professionals with highly diverse backgrounds and areas of expertise, the premise has remained that there is a need and a right to beauty. From ink drawings on linen, to sophisticated computer documentation, the process of communication and resolution has been consistently focused on contributing to the well being of the people for whom we toil.

These five decades have been similar only in the vagaries with which they are in retrospect defined. Societal, regulatory, financial, and technological determinants have both impinged upon, and positively influenced, our architecture. We remain unable to design external to the boundaries of the ever changing culture to which we belong; and our work reflects the time in which it was authored.

In the decade after World War II our work reflected the tenets of Modernism. An aesthetic responsive to function, but one tempered by a truly deep sensitivity to the interplay between structure and environment. It was architecture which became increasingly refined, as it grew increasingly complex. The simple but elegant interplay of planes and volumes which describe the Peaslee Beach House, becomes a richly layered composition as Lankenau Hospital.

The 1960's were a time of significant growth in our practice. The institutional sector which had formed the focus of our work was complemented by significantly increased commissions from the corporate realm. We were designing buildings for universities, hospitals, and the Federal Government; and corporate headquarters, studios, and stadia. Urban renewal proposals addressed conditions in Philadelphia, Pittsburgh, and Washington, D.C. And in 1969 Kling absorbed an affiliated engineering firm, to become one of very few practices offering engineering design as well as architecture.

By the early 1970's we were one of the largest architectural firms in the country. At this time we were actively involved in the re-creation of Center City Philadelphia, so that even today much of what one understands as the city's identity is our work; as are many of the pedestrian areas — the plazas, fountains, concourses, and urban gardens. The mid-1970's are exemplified by monumental architecture. The two million square foot headquarters for ATT which employed roof forms to be respectful to surrounding residential neighborhoods, and Bell Laboratories facility which used a similar approach to integrate the building with the landscape were precursors of work to come. The University of Connecticut, Scheie Eye Institute, and International Monetary Fund celebrated the plastic qualities of concrete in deeply expressive enclosures which remain important edifices in their respective contexts.

We began the next ten year period with multiple projects for national corporations including Prudential and Merrill Lynch; buildings as singular responses to their unique settings. At the same time we were establishing increasing expertise in areas predicated on technology — research and development laboratories, computer centers, and government facilities which necessitated both architectural and engineering skills and inventiveness.

The most recent decade is that represented by the work included in this monograph. It is architecture with great diversity in scale and program, purpose and presentation, expectation and resolution. It is architecture which remains completely committed to the issues of social responsibility and the advocacy of artistry upon which the practice was founded.

Selected Projects
1945-1988

1945 – 1959

1945 - Peaslee Beach House
Mantloking, New Jersey

1953 - Lankenau Hospital
Master Plan & Seven Buildings
Overbrook, Pennsylvania

1955 - Radio Corporation of America
Offices & Plant
Cherry Hill, New Jersey

1958 - Harriton High School
Rosemont, Pennsylvania

1960 – 1969

1961 - Concordia College
Masterplan & All Buildings
Ann Arbor, Michigan

1962 - American Baptist Convention
Headquarters Building
Valley Forge, Pennsylvania

1963 - Triangle Publication, Inc.
Channel 6 Broadcast Studio
Philadelphia, Pennsylvania

1965 - Armstrong, Inc.
Philadelphia, Pennsylvania

1969 - E.I. DuPont de Nemours & Co.
Brandywine Highrise Building
Wilmington, Delaware

1970 – 1979

1974 - Bell Laboratories
Murray Hill, New Jersey

**1974 - Center Square at City Hall &
Municipal Services Building**
Philadelphia, Pennsylvania

1976 - International Monetary Fund
Washington, District of Columbia

1979 - Sheie Eye Institute
Philadelphia, Pennsylvania

1980 – 1988

1980 - Connelly Center
Villanova University
Villanova Pennsylvania

1981 - Prudential Insurance Co.
Regional Headquarters
Roseland, New Jersey

1985 - Boehringer Ingelheim, Ltd.
Research Laboratory Complex
Danbury, CT

1985 - Cargill, Inc.
Corporate Headquarters
Minnetonka, Minnesota

1985 - Merrill Lynch
Training Center
Princeton, New Jersey

Project Credits 1989-1999

LEBOW ENGINEERING CENTER
Client: Drexel University
Design Principal: Eric Chung
Managing Principal: Charles Bailey
Project Manager: Gene Spurgeon
Project Architect: Peter Dustin
Design Team: Bradford Fiske,
Chuck Gantt, Joseph Reagan,
Kerry Gingrich, Sue Hu
Structural Engineers: Kling Lindquist
MEP Engineers: Kling Lindquist
Civil / Landscape: Kling Lindquist
Interior Design: Kling Lindquist
Photographer: C. Geoffrey Berken

BELL ATLANTIC TOWER
Client: Bell Atlantic Properties
Design Principal: Bradford Fiske
Managing Principal: Jack Rutkowski
Senior Designer: David Doelp
Project Manager: Richard Farley
Project Architects: Thomas Hoos,
Joseph Reagan
Design Team: David Bader, Alfred Bell,
David Colman, Chris Silver,
Witold Wituchowski
Structural Engineers: CBM
MEP Engineers: Cosentini Associates
Civil / Landscape: Kling Lindquist:
Paul Neyhart
Photographer: Timothy Hursley

BAYER KYOTO PHARMACEUTICAL RESEARCH CENTER COMPETITION
Client: Bayer AG
Design Principal: Eric Chung
Design Team: Roy Decker,
Bradford Fiske, David Kenyon,
Dana von Goetz

LEWIS J. BLUEMLE JR. LIFE SCIENCES BUILDING
Client: Thomas Jefferson University
Design Principal: Eric Chung
Managing Principal: Jack Rutkowski
Project Manager: Charles Bailey

Project Architect: Sungman Paik
Design Team: Robert Little,
Serm Permsa, Anatole Persicky
*Structural Engineers:*Kling Lindquist
MEP Engineers: Kling Lindquist
Civil / Landscape: Kling Lindquist
Photographer: C. Geoffrey Berken

GLAXO PHARMACEUTICAL R&D HEADQUARTERS COMPLEX
Client: Glaxo Inc. USA
Design Principals: Binh Vinh,
Eric Chung
*Managing Principal:*Melvyn J. Sotnick
Project Managers: Helmut
Krohnemann, Ken Gardiner
Project Architects: Ray Donovan,
Wolf Pohl, William Reichert,
John Robinson, John Suter
Design Team: Lou Angelus, Yu-Chien
Ann, Stefan Boens, Peter Brown,
Mariette Buchman, Ken DuBois,
Harry Dumesnil, Harold Grote,
Raj Halankar, Sue Hu,
John LaProcido, David Manty,
Jeff Phuhl, Ron Salutric, Jeff Wu
Structural Engineers: Kling Lindquist:
Joseph Cuilla, Doug Henderson,
Anthony Ercole
MEP Engineers: Kling Lindquist:
Michael Lorenz
Civil / Landscape: Kling Lindquist:
Chris Rummler, David Ostrich,
John Zeambaugh
*Interior Design:*Kling Lindquist:
Mary Gale, David Oess, Chris Wirkkala
Photographers: Jerry Blow, Peter Paige,
James Steinkamp

STERLING WINTHROP R&D HEADQUARTERS COMPLEX
Client: Sterling Winthrop Inc.
Design Principal: Eric Chung
Managing Principal: Robert Thompson
Senior Designer: Robert Little
Project Managers: Michael Koluch,
John Neilson, Andy Schoerke,

Richard Mang, Michael Timmons
Project Architects: William Haus,
James Kennon, Michael Petulla,
Ellen Prantel
Design Team: Lou Angelus,
Mariette Buchman, David Bader,
Mark Clearwood,
Anthony Golebiewski, Gregg Olmstead
Martin Sharpless, Anthony Sinisi
Jaime Rouillon, Hans Warner,
Chris Silver
Structural Engineers: Kling Lindquist:
Girard Gioia, George Hughes
MEP Engineers: Kling Lindquist:
Patrick Carpenter, Frank Klusek,
Robert Roth, Charles Rowland
Civil/Landscape: Kling Lindquist:
Joseph Cuilla, Louis Dibello,
Joseph Lucas
Interior Design: Kling Lindquist:
David Oess
Photographer: C. Geoffrey Berken

MERCK PRODUCT RESEARCH AND DEVELOPMENT FACILITY (BUILDING 78)
Client: Merck & Co., Inc.
Design Principal: Bradford Fiske
Managing Principals: Jack Rutkowski,
Robert Thompson
Project Manager: Helmut Krohnemann
Project Architect: Joseph Tinari
Design Team: Gregg Olmstead,
Grazyna Samborska, G.T. Tang
Structural Engineers: Kling Lindquist:
Doug Henderson
MEP Engineers: Kling Lindquist:
Dennis Brooks, Scott Davis
Civil / Landscape: Kling Lindquist:
Joseph Cuilla, Louis DiBello
Interior Design: Kling Lindquist:
Florinda Doelp
Photographers: C. Geoffrey Berken,
Matt Wargo

GLAXO WELLCOME MEDICINES RESEARCH CENTER
Client: Glaxo Wellcome p.l.c.
Design Principal: Binh Vinh
Managing Principal: Alexander Ralston
Project Managers: George Cole,
Robert Kumlin, Richard Mang,
Jeffrey Matthews, Gene Spurgeon,
Project Architect: Cynthia Brey,
John Robinson
Design Team: Joon Chung,
Guilla Finta,William Gariano,
Harold Grote, Huy Nguyen,
Dan Watch, Michael Yetterberg
Associate Architect: Sheppard Robson
Structural Engineers:
KlingLindquist/Ove Arup
MEP Engineers:
Kling Lindquist/ Ove Arup
Landscape Architect: Gillespies:
Scott Bowers, Randy Nofs
Photographer: Dennis Gilbert

QVC CORPORATE HEADQUARTERS COMPETITION
Client: QVC
Design Principal: Bradford Fiske
Design Collaborators:
Christine Bacha-Rizk, Cathy Dopkin,
Marc Fischer, Marcello Franganillo,
Jonathan Ginnis, Sue Hu,
Cory Hunnicut, Robert Little,
Chris Rummler, Lillian Sung

UNITED STATES FOOD AND DRUG ADMINISTRATION HEADQUARTERS CONSOLIDATION
Client: USFDA/GSA
Design Principals: Eric Chung,
Bradford Fiske
Managing Principals:
Alexander Ralston, Lewis Robinson
Senior Designer: Stan Andrulis
Project Manager: Gene Spurgeon,
Michael Timmons

Project Architect: Richard Brown
Design Team: John Robinson,
Matthew Romano, Justin Seto,
Larry Wolford
Associate Architect: RTKL
Structural Engineers: Kling Lindquist
MEP Engineers: Kling Lindquist
Civil Engineers:
Greenhorn O'Mara

GLAXO FRANCE ADMINISTRATIVE HEADQUARTERS
Client: Glaxo
Design Principal: Eric Chung
Managing Principal: Noel Fagerlund
Design Team: Christine Bacha-Rizk,
Bradford Fiske, Rick Focke,
Chris Rummler, Mark Schlenker,
Dan Watch
Associate Architect:
Synthese Architecture
Structural Engineers: Groupe S.E.E.E.
MEP Engineers: Groupe S.E.E.E.
Photographer: Eric Chung

SHENZHEN TELEVISION CENTER
Client: City of Shenzhen, China
Design Principal: Bradford Fiske
Design Collaborators:
Alberto Cavallero, Kelly Dapra,
Marcello Franganillo, Sue Hu,
Qingyun Ma, Kami Olmstead,
Peter Vierra, William Weber,
Jonathan Weiss

SHENZHEN CULTURAL CENTER
Client: City of Shenzhen, China
Design Principal: Bradford Fiske
Design Collaborators:
Christine Bacha-Rizk,
Alberto Cavallero, Kelly Dapra,
Marcello Franganillo, Sue Hu,
Els Leen, Qingyun Ma,
Clarissa Mendez, Griet Sinnaeve,
Mathew Xavier

8 6 1 9

CENTER CITY OFFICE TOWER
Client: Withheld
Design Principal: Bradford Fiske
Design Team: Alberto Cavallero,
Curt Dilger, Marcello Franganillo,
Qingyun Ma

DOW JONES CORPORATE OFFICE FACILITY
Client: Dow Jones & Co., Inc.
Design Principal: Bradford Fiske
Managing Principal: Richard Farley
Senior Designer: David Doelp
Project Architect: John Suter
Design Team: Christine Bacha-Rizk,
Joon Chung, Marcello Franganillo,
Sue Hu, Robert Little, Paul Marchese,
Ken Vogel, Jonathan Weiss
Structural Engineers: Kling Lindquist:
Richard Rowe, Paul Hobelmann
MEP Engineers: Kling Lindquist:
Michael Lorenz, Frank Nemia,
Robert Roth
Civil Engineers: Kling Lindquist:
Joseph Cuilla, Lupin Ahmed
Landscape Architect: Kling Lindquist:
Chris Rummler, Robert Maloney
Interior Design: Kling Lindquist:
Richard Mark, Anthony Saby
Photographer: Jeff Goldberg/ESTO

MERCK MULTI-SCIENCE FACILITY (BUILDING 800)
Client: Merck & Co., Inc.
Design Principal: Bradford Fiske
Managing Principal: Robert Thompson
Senior Designer: Robert Little
Project Manager: John Neilson,
Ken Schotsch
Project Architect: Joseph Tinari
Design Team: Bruce Arnold,
Christine Bacha-Rizk, Robert Myer,
Ellen Sisle, Lillian Sung,
Jonathan Weiss
Structural Engineers: Kling Lindquist:
Richard Rowe, Gerard Gioia
MEP Engineers: Kling Lindquist:

Michael Lorenz, Dennis Brooks,
Jon Hofmeister, Salvatore Gugliotta
Civil Engineers: Kling Lindquist:
Joseph Cuilla, John Kostyo
Landscape Architect: Kling Lindquist:
Chris Rummler, Thomas Grahame
Interior Design: Kling Lindquist:
Richard Mark, Anthony Saby,
Michelle Banfe

SAP AMERICA, INC. HEADQUARTERS
Client: SAP America, Inc.
Design Principal: Bradford Fiske
Managing Principal: Richard Farley
Senior Project Architect: Joseph Castner
Project Manager: Helmut Krohnemann
Design Team: Alberto Cavallero,
Kelly Dapra, Marcello Franganillo,
Els Leen, Shouning Li, Qingyun Ma,
Louis Poupon, Gerry Power,
Lillian Sung, Addis Valentine,
Jonathan Weiss
Structural Engineers: Kling Lindquist:
Richard Rowe, Paul Hobelmann
MEP Engineers: Kling Lindquist:
Michael Lorenz, Donald Tangarone,
John Toy
Civil/Landscape: Kling Lindquist:
Joseph Cuilla, Chris Rummler,
Nicole Suka, David Traczykiewicz,
Tim Gardner
Interior Design: Studios
Photographer: Jeff Goldberg/ESTO